Peace and Re
in Internatio
Islamic Law

"Kaleem Hussain's book is an important scholarly contribution to the literature available on peace, reconciliation and conflict resolution, with diplomatic sensitivities in the context of International Law and Islamic Law. International humanitarian law and laws of war can learn a lot from Islamic history, which is replete with shining examples of mercy, forgiveness, generosity and chivalry.

Given the struggles of the people of Kashmir and Palestine, and so many other unresolved conflicts, Kaleem Hussain's work is essential reading as it provides a scholarly perspective on the interface of International Law and Islamic Law, whose principles can make deft diplomacy and peace and reconciliation a force multiplier for a rules-based world order, which is the bedrock of international relations."

Senator Mushahid Hussain Sayed
Journalist, Politician, and Chairman of the Senate Defence Committee in Pakistan

"Kaleem Hussain offers smart, realistic and achievable solutions for a world torn apart by bitter grievances and conflict, and his thoughtful and evidence-based ideas deserve the widest audience. Drawn from a careful reading of history, and especially from Islamic Law and tradition, he has identified and beautifully explained key proven processes for de-escalating problems and restoring harmony."

Dr. Joel Hayward
Professor of Strategic Thought, Rabdan Academy, United Arab Emirates

"This book is a laudable contribution to the study of its very important and timely topic."

Dr. Ahmed Al-Dawoody,
Legal Adviser for Islamic Law and Jurisprudence at the International Committee of the Red Cross (ICRC)

"Hussain explores the intersections of diplomacy and International Law from the under-utilised lens of Shari'a principles. With conflict ravaging Muslim-majority countries, this timely book raises the issue of what role an Islamic approach too peace building might play."

Dr. Nasya Bahfen
Senior Lecturer in Journalism, La Trobe University, Australia

Peace and Reconciliation in International and Islamic Law

By
Kaleem Hussain

Peace and Reconciliation in International and Islamic Law

By Kaleem Hussain

This book was first published in hardback in 2023 by Cambridge Scholars Publishing

The current paperback version has been independently published in 2023

Copyright © 2023 by Kaleem Hussain

All rights for this book reserved. No part of this book may be reproduced, stored in a retrieval system, or transmitted, in any form or by any means, electronic, mechanical, photocopying, recording or otherwise, without the prior permission of the copyright owner.

ISBN: 9798850616403

I dedicate this book to my wife and daughter who have continuously motivated me throughout the book's journey for which I am grateful, my beloved parents whose love, affection and grace one is forever indebted to, my comrades, friends and leaders in society whose courage and determination are utterly inspirational and to those around the world who are suffering under injustice and oppression.

Disclaimer: when it comes to hadith citation, the author has not referred directly to the primary hadith source but has relied on the authoritative citation cited in the books and articles consulted that are mentioned in the reference section.

The viewpoints expressed by the author in this book are that of the author and do not in any way represent the viewpoints of the organisations the author has affiliations with currently or previously.

TABLE OF CONTENTS

Acknowledgments viii

Introduction 1

Chapter One... 5
Conflict Resolution, Arbitration, and Peacekeeping/ Building based
on Sources of Public International Law
    Conflict Resolution 6
    Arbitration 8
    The International Court of Justice (ICJ) Evidence 9
    Evidence.. 13
    Remedies 13
    Advisory Jurisdiction of the Court 14
    Conciliation 14
    International Institution Dispute Settlement 15
    Use of Force.. 16
    The Right of Self Defence: Article 51................................... 16
    Civil Wars 18
    International Humanitarian Law 19
    Nuclear Weapons 22
    Armed Conflicts- International and Internal Dimensions.... 23
    International Human Rights Law... 24

Chapter Two 32
Conflict Resolution, Arbitration, and Peacekeeping/Building Based
on Sources of Islamic Law
    The Concept of Peace in International Islamic Law............ 32
    Islamic Legal Sources on Peace and Reconciliation 34
    Counter Terrorism within the Islamic Tradition.................. 36
    Sanctity, Safety and Protection of Missing Persons............. 40
    Diplomacy Within the Islamic Tradition.............................. 42
    Rebellion 44
    Conflicts Between Two Equal Parties................................... 4

Chapter Three 49
A Comparative Analysis of Peace, Reconciliation, Conflict Resolution and
Arbitration Based on Sources of Public International and Islamic Law
    Islamic Law and International law *49*
    Difference *51*
    Custom *53*
    Rule of Law Convergence *54*
    Divergence from Peace *54*
    International Islamic Law: Perceptions and Reality *56*
    Peace and Reconciliation in Islamic and International Law *58*
    Conflict Resolution and Arbitration in Islamic and International
       Law *59*
    International Islamic Law (siyar) *60*
    Counter Terrorism and Security Based on Sources of Public
       International Law and International Islamic Law *61*
    Treating Prisoners of War, Hostages according to Islamic
       International law and Public International law *62*
       Protection of Civilians and Non-Combatants 62
       Protection of Property 63
       Military Property: The Objective is Surrender 63
       Treatment of Prisoners 64
    International Legal System (ILS) and International Peaceful
       Resolution Methods *69*
    Islamic Collectives and Just Ordered Community *69*
    Dialogue and Diplomacy based on Islamic Humanitarian Law
       and International Humanitarian Law *70*
    Use of Force According to Public and Islamic International Law *71*
    Human Rights and Humanitarians According to Public and
       International Islamic Law *71*

Chapter Four 76
Peace and Reconciliation in Practice
    Afghanistan *77*
    Palestine/Israel *85*
    Kashmir *95*
    Towards a Theo-Diplomacy Paradigm *102*

Chapter Five 111
Conclusion

Notes... 122

ACKNOWLEDGMENTS

As a humble student and observer of international relations and the Islamic tradition, I would like to acknowledge my limitations across multiple fronts in this endeavour. I extend special thanks and appreciation to those who have contributed in my journey to write this book. In particular, to Senator Mushahid Hussain Syed, Jamil Zubairi, Professor Ahmed Al-Dawoody, Professor Emilia Justyna Powell, Jonathan Kuttab, Professor Joel Hayward and Professor Akbar Ahmed who spared their valuable time to answer my interview questions.

I am moreover indebted to Dr Nasya Bahfen and all the reviewers of the manuscript at Cambridge Scholars Publishing whose feedback and comments proved invaluable in refining my thoughts.

MAPS

Palestine-Israel

Kashmir

Afghanistan

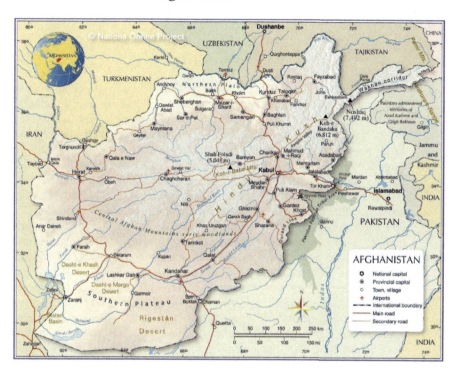

Country political maps provided courtesy of Nations Online Project.
https://www.nationsonline.org/

Introduction

Abstract

This chapter sets out the core premise of the book. This book introduces a new theological approach to international law and dispute settlement, drawing from the rich tradition of Islamic law. This new approach refines the tools that are available to international interlocutors to help arbitrate and foster peace and reconciliation between disputing parties. It also sets the stage for exploring the potentials and pitfalls of such a theological model for international conflict resolution, peace and reconciliation initiatives.

We inhabit a world that is deeply interconnected. In this kind of global order, multiple jurisdictions, international treaties, frameworks, conventions, and international norms are used and indeed *required*. These instruments help to resolve conflicts between nation states, establish peace, and reconcile issues between several international actors. In this context, the aim of this book is to shed light on the *normative principles of theological jurisprudence*—which can provide a new basis for negotiating these large-scale international disputes and working towards peace and reconciliation. While the parameters of public international law provide the legal framework for the conduct of nation states in conflicts and wars, I shall demonstrate here that supplementing these legal tools with a theological approach can assist the mechanisms of arbitration and peacekeeping to broker peaceful outcomes. This new approach—grounded in theology and informed by the developments of the modern world—has much to add to conflict resolution at a global scale.

It can be noted, of course, that such a theological basis often leads to conflict and stalemate in the first place and fuels global and regional disputes of a religious character. From this viewpoint, a *neutral* theological framework is best suited to broker a peaceful resolution to a conflict. I shall demonstrate what such a *neutral* theological framework would entail. I shall then show that while a theologically neutral jurisdictional framework can indeed be useful as a tool for conflict resolution, if these frameworks do not address the sensitive theological issues that drive certain conflicts, then they are less likely to succeed in resolving those conflicts.

This book brings a novel perspective to the peaceful resolution of disputes, as understood under the framework of international law. International law—or the way we see it today—is a product of a range of historic and cultural events. The birth of this legal system on a global scale can be traced to the systematic creation of international *institutions* in the post-world war era. Institutions such as the United Nations and its organs, including the World Bank, the World Trade Organization, the International Monetary Fund, and several other bodies, were created to achieve harmony, international peace, and cooperation between nation-states.

The faith in the power of these institutions—often termed *institutionalism*—is a core perspective in international law. One prominent tussle is between the *realists* and the *institutionalists*. Whereas the realists are sceptical about the role that these institutions can play in achieving cooperation (owing to power imbalances and the vested interests of nation-states), institutionalists see cooperation through systematic mechanisms from within the folds of international law as a real and achievable possibility. These two opposing narratives seem to frame early approaches to international law.

Another dominant framework, which has gained traction with time, is the 'liberal perspective' to international law. The liberals adopt what has been called a 'bottom-up' approach, by emphasising that every state is rooted in an interdependent transitional society and polity and thus it is in the interest of nation-states to achieve cooperation and maintain global order. In contrast—or perhaps at least in a different vein—there are perspectives such as *constructivism* that seek not to adopt a particular political conception of international law, but instead to question how international law facilitates and contributes to a unique set of social norms.

Born from these constructivist developments (and perhaps in opposition to them), the period after the Second World War brought a new critical perspective to international law to the forefront—'third world approaches to international law' or 'TWAIL', as such theories are often called. TWAIL scholars see international law as a system that *legitimatises the power imbalance* of Western powers with colonial histories over the Global South. They argue for a 'decolonisation' of international law. Born of this general critical vein, we also see new perspectives to international law, including feminist, post-structuralist, and Marxist perspectives to international law and theory.

Considering these several perspectives and their development over time and context, we require a theoretical framework that reconciles these approaches—not in the abstract, but in terms of *contextual particulars*. Our theory must arise from and be informed by the realities of global conflict, and not vice versa. It is with this commitment that this book proceeds. I hope to develop a perspective to international law that is informed by the particularities and nuances of context-specific readings of Islamic law. I shall demonstrate, through the findings of this book, that the core principles of the latter can provide a novel and valuable perspective with which to see the former.

In some ways, this project may seem to align well with the constructivist aims: by examining the social norms that emerge when we think of international law, from a lens of theological jurisprudence. It also has a general liberal commitment—by seeking to uphold peace, cooperation, and stability among individual states. This project could also be seen as a critical project that aligns with TWAIL because it draws from Islamic, non-dominant perspectives that are born out of the Global South. However, instead of seeing the Global South as a monolith or being committed to any particular political ideology, this book is set in the context of several real-world challenges. It draws from the realities of theatres of conflict across the world to show that Islamic law can help pave the way for peacebuilding and dispute-resolution under international law and policy.

In Chapter 1, I lay down the core principles of international law and provide a brief overview of peacebuilding and conflict resolution mechanisms under public international law.

In Chapter 2, I turn to Islamic Law and discuss the main principles of Islamic law before elaborating on the notions of peacebuilding as codified under Islamic law. Chapter 3 then undertakes a rigorous comparative analysis that draws from the material in the preceding chapters. I provide a comparative analysis of international law and Islamic law—discussing the many points of divergence, and importantly, of convergence between the two legal approaches.

The discussion in these three chapters sets the stage for Chapter 4, wherein I apply the findings on the confluence between international law and Islamic law to three major sites of geo-political conflict—Afghanistan, Israel and Palestine, and Kashmir. I focus on these three sites or 'theatres' of conflict because of their deep and complex connections with Islamic law and because of the prevalence of Islamic law in the regions that these disputes affect. I show that understanding these conflicts through the *intersection* of Islamic law and international law can help reframe and resolve core conflict points and pave the way for peaceful resolution of these disputes.

My analysis of these conflict sites also allows for a more general framing of the intersections between Islamic law and international law—by developing an approach that I theorise calling 'theo-diplomacy.' After outlining the contours of such an approach in Chapter 4, I elaborate on the potentials and future avenues of this approach in the concluding section of the book.

One hopes that this book will be of benefit to think-tanks; inter-faith institutions; government departments; diplomats, ambassadors, statesmen and stateswomen; consulates; faith leaders; universities; public policy and political science departments; international relations analysts; counter terrorism and security experts; and academics. I hope that these stakeholders—all uniquely placed at the several intersections of international law, policy, and practice—will benefit from engaging with the core insights and claims made in this book. Taken together, this book aims to provide a neutral conflict resolution framework, rooted equally in faith-based understandings from Islamic law and the principles of dispute resolution and peace that frame international law and policy.

CHAPTER ONE

CONFLICT RESOLUTION, ARBITRATION, AND
PEACEKEEPING/PEACEBUILDING BASED ON
SOURCES OF PUBLIC INTERNATIONAL LAW

Abstract

This chapter addresses some of the prime sources and procedures available in international law for the peaceful resolution of disputes and conflicts. It particularly focuses on how international law relates with conflict resolution, arbitration, peacekeeping, and building. It is important to note, preliminarily, that the international approach to these three discrete elements incorporates standardised universal norms. The comity of nations is required to abide by these norms, along with specific instructions directed at regions and nation states. As these norms are at the very centre of international law's *modus operandi*, international law itself sees its purpose as the establishment and maintenance of global peace and security."[1] Article 2 (3) of the United Nations Charter states, in a similar vein, that: "[A]ll members shall settle their international disputes by peaceful means in such a manner that international peace and security and justice are not endangered."[2] The peaceful settlement of large-scale international disputes seems to thus be a core principle in international law.

There are several mechanisms available to states who are seeking settlement of international disputes. As stated in the 1970 *Declaration on Principles of International Law Concerning Friendly Relations and Co-operation among States*:

> "The parties to any dispute, the continuance of which is likely to endanger the maintenance of international peace and security, shall, first of all, seek a solution by negotiation, inquiry, mediation, conciliation, arbitration, judicial settlement, resort to regional agencies or arrangements or other peaceful means of their choice."[3]

This chapter provides an overview of these mechanisms for the just settlement of disputes under international law. It is my aim that this overview will set the stage for a comparative and theoretical discussion of the link between international law and Islamic law in the subsequent parts of this book.

Conflict Resolution

Conflict resolution is one of the core principles of international law. This is the mechanism for resolving differences of opinion or postures that either have or may instigate a conflict, by applying reconciliation and resolution mechanisms between the relevant parties to arrive at an amicable resolution. It is important to note that states, however, are *not obligated* to resolve their differences. The methods and mechanisms that are available to settle disputes require the consent of the states themselves. This is a key point that shows how important the consent of states is in the framework of conflict resolution under international law.

Note that this is not the case for Security Council Resolutions, which are binding in their application.[4] As Article 25 of the UN Charter states:

> The Members of the United Nations agree to accept and carry out the decisions of the Security Council in accordance with the present Charter.[5]

With the exception of these decisions, however, states must consent (and are not bound) to resolve their differences through available mechanisms under international law.

Furthermore, disputes can fragment into legal or political disagreements that can be either justiciable or non-justiciable.[6] As a result, political and legal organs often deal with aspects of the same legal or political situations.[7] Parties to a dispute have an obligation to seek a settlement by alternative means, which must be agreed by all parties, in the event that a method fails. If a specific approach fails to resolve a dispute, and the continuation of that dispute is likely to endanger the maintenance of international peace and security, Article 37 (1) of the Charter stipulates that the parties shall refer it to the Security Council.[8]

A key precondition to reconciling conflicts and differences is meaningful and purposeful negotiation. Negotiations often require parties to compromise certain elements of their position to arrive at a peaceful resolution and require that one party takes the initiative to negotiate. The importance of consultation is endorsed by Article 84 of the Vienna Convention on the Representation of States, which stipulates that if a dispute arises between parties owing to the interpretation of the convention, any party can request consultations to resolve the dispute.[9]

There is nothing specific in the Charter, or under international law, that stipulates a rule to the effect that exhausting diplomatic negotiations is a pretext for a matter to be referred to the court. Tribunals can direct parties to engage in negotiations in good faith and may stipulate the factors that need to be considered in the course of negotiations between the parties. A key prerequisite when states resort to negotiations is that they should negotiate meaningfully, with a view to arriving at an early settlement that is acceptable to both parties.[10]

Another aspect of conflict resolution is that of the inquiry. Where a difference of opinion exists on factual matters related to a dispute between parties, the preferred solution is to institute a commission or inquiry, managed by reputable observers, to identify accurately which facts and issues are in contention. Such provisions were first proposed in the 1899 Hague Conference as an alternative to arbitration. As David Caron notes:

> The 1899 Peace Conference was a point of inflection, a turn in the river, in the effort to move beyond ad hoc international arbitration to adjudication by a permanent international court as a means to avoid war and preserve international peace and security.[11]

There are, however, limitations to the inquiry process envisaged here. An inquiry can possess relevance only in the case of international disputes that involve neither the honour nor the vital interests of the parties, and where the particular disagreement at stake can be resolved via recourse to an impartial and conscientious investigation.[12]

The importance of inquiries within specific institutional frameworks is clear: they have been used, in particular, with the United Nations and by specialist agencies. For instance, consider the UN Secretary General Mission in 1988 to Iran and Iraq to investigate the situation of prisoners of war, at the request of those states (S/20147). Or we may recall the UN Compensation Commission, which was set up to resolve claims against Iraq resulting from its invasion of Kuwait in 1990. This was described by the UN Secretary General as performing an "essentially fact-finding function."[13] Such mechanisms, however, can discourage states. As Shaw notes:

> "In many disputes, of course, the determination of the relevant circumstances would simply not aid a settlement, whilst its nature as a third-party involvement in a situation would discourage some states." [14]

Thus, despite its limitations, the inquiry or commission process continues to be an effective procedure to identify facts and issues at stake in a dispute.

Arbitration

Other than conflict resolution through these means, arbitration is also an option available to states to peacefully settle their disputes. The 1970 Declaration on Principles of International Law Concerning Friendly Relations and Co-operation states that:

> States shall accordingly seek early and just settlement of their international disputes by negotiation, inquiry, mediation, conciliation, arbitration, judicial settlement, resort to regional agencies or arrangements or other peaceful means of their choice.[15]

Article 33 (1) of the UN Charter discusses disputes that are likely to endanger international peace and security. It stipulates that states have a free choice regarding the mechanisms adopted for settling their disputes in these cases.[16]

A key characteristic of arbitration is the principle of good faith, which includes refraining from obstructive behaviour during the negotiation process. This point was emphasised by the International Court when it addressed the legality of either the threat or use of nuclear weapons."[17] Third parties play a crucial role here. In all arbitration proceedings, a third-party mediator applies the "good office" role to encourage contending parties to reach a settlement. Unlike the technique of adjudication, the process aims to persuade the parties to reach satisfactory terms for the termination of a dispute by themselves; the provisions for settling the dispute are not prescribed.[18] An example of the effective use of the good office function was performed by the USSR in assisting in the peaceful settlement of the India–Pakistan dispute in 1965. As well as through collaboration with office holders or regional organisations, the UN Secretary General can, on occasion, play a key role by exercising the good office Declarations on the Prevention and Removal of Disputes in situations which may threaten international peace and security.[19]

The *1899 Hague Convention for the Pacific Settlement of Disputes* includes several provisions on international arbitration, the object of which, under Article 15, was deemed to be "the settlement of differences between states by judges of their own choice and on the basis of respect for law."[20] An agreement to arbitrate under Article 18 implies the legal obligation to accept the terms of the award. In addition, a Permanent Court of Arbitration was established. This court is not a court in the usual sense, because it is not composed of a fixed body of judges. It consists of a panel of persons, nominated by the contracting states (each one nominating a maximum of four), and including individuals "of known competency in questions of international law, of the highest moral reputation and disposed to accept the duties of an arbitrator."[21]

One of the key components of arbitration is that of observing independence and impartiality. States are not obliged to submit a dispute to the procedure of arbitration. In the absence of their consent, several treaties primarily dealing with the peaceful settlement of disputes have declined in importance since 1945. The question of consent or compromise, or of special agreement, and the terms in which they are couched, are significant in determining how the arbitration process will work.

The law applied in arbitration proceedings is international law, but the parties may agree on certain principles to be considered by the tribunal and specify this in the compromise, such as the principles of law and equity.

There are also Rules of Procedures to be followed as part of arbitration. The *Hague Convention* of 1889, as revised in 1907, contains agreed procedural principles, which would apply in the absence of express stipulation:

> It is characteristic of arbitration that the tribunal is competent to determine its own jurisdiction and therefore interpret the relevant instruments determining that jurisdiction.[22]

Arbitration as a method of settling disputes combines elements of both diplomatic and judicial procedures. Its success in resolving disputes depends on a certain amount of goodwill between the parties in drawing up the compromise, constituting the tribunal, and enforcing the subsequent award.[23] Arbitration is an adjudicative technique in that the award is final and binding, and the arbitrators are required to base their decision on law. Considering its similarities with the process of judicial settlement, the Permanent Court of Arbitration began to decline with the establishment and consolidation of the Permanent Court of International Justice in the 1920s.

However, despite this, arbitration continues to be an extremely useful process in cases wherein some specific technical expertise is required. Or furthermore, in cases where the parties despite greater flexibility and speed than what the International Court can provide them, arbitration once again becomes an attractive option.[24]

The International Court of Justice (ICJ)

Together with the mechanism of arbitration, the Permanent Court of International Justice (PCIJ) was established to provide a comprehensive system of dispute-settlement that served the interests of the international community. Although there are several international and regional courts that are available to decide disputes in accordance with the rules and principles of international law, the most prestigious of these is certainly the International Court of Justice (ICJ). We shall now discuss the processes and functions of this court briefly to gauge its significance.

After the Second World War, Article 92 of the Charter established the ICJ as the "Principal Judicial Organ" of the United Nations. It was intended to prevent outbreaks of violence by providing freely accessible methods of dispute settlement. The ICJ is a continuation of the Permanent Court, with the same statute and jurisdiction, and with continuity in the line of cases; no distinction is made between those decided by the PCIJ and by the ICJ.[25] Article 2 of the Statute of the ICJ stipulates that it is composed of 15 members:

> Elected regardless of their nationality, from among persons of high moral character, who possess the qualifications required in their respective countries for appointment to the highest judicial offices or are juriconsults of recognised competence in International Law.[26]

The ICJ decides cases based on international law as it stands at the date of the decision. It cannot formally create law as it is not a legislative organ. As part of the ICJ's *modus operandi*, it is important to note that disputes are resolved in accordance with international law, and that the court refrains from adjudicating on points that are not included in the final submissions of the parties. Article 36 (2) of the Statute of the Court requires that matters before it should be a legal dispute.[27] A legal dispute, has roughly been defined by the Court, as "a disagreement over a point of law or fact, a conflict of legal views or of interests between two persons."[28] Furthermore, in the *Interpretation of the Peace Treaties Case*, the Court noted that "whether there exists an international dispute is a matter for objective determination" and further pointed out that in the present case "the two sides hold clearly opposite views concerning the question of the performance or the non-performance of certain treaty obligations so that international disputes have risen."[29] The Court also specified that for a matter to constitute a legal dispute, it is sufficient for the respondent to an application before the Court merely to deny the allegations, even if the jurisdiction of the Court is challenged.[30]

Another vital component to international arbitration is jurisdiction—having the capacity to decide disputes between states, and the capacity to provide advisory opinions when requested so to do by qualified entities.[31] Article 36 (6) sets out the competence of the court to determine its own jurisdiction. In the *Fisheries Jurisdiction (Spain v Canada)* case, it was held that while the party alleging a matter of fact has to prove said fact before the Court, the issue of jurisdiction is a *question of law* which can only be determined by the Court.[32] Once the court has reached a decision on jurisdiction, that decision assumes the character of *res judicata*—it is final and binding upon the parties to the dispute.[33] It is important to emphasise that the absence of jurisdiction to resolve disputes about compliance with a particular obligation under international law does not affect the existence and binding force of that obligation. As the court has stressed as part of international humanitarian law and international human rights law, states are required to fulfil their obligations under international law, and they remain responsible for acts contrary to international law which are attributable to them. The Court has jurisdiction under Article 36 (1) of its Statute in all cases referred to it by the parties, and regarding all matters specially provided for in the UN Charter or in treaties or conventions in force.[34] As in the case of arbitration, parties may refer a particular dispute to the ICJ by means of a special agreement or compromise, which will specify the terms of the dispute and the framework within which the Court is to operate. This method was utilised in the Minquiers and Ecrehos case, as well as in several others.[35] In matters pertaining to the Jurisdiction of the court and the consent of the parties, the court can also infer this from the conduct of the parties. For instance, consider the *Corfu Chanel* (Preliminary Objections) case, wherein consent was inferred from the actions and conduct of the plaintiff in that case—the United Kingdom—despite the absence of explicit agreement or consent to submit to the Court's jurisdiction. Although the Court does indeed make such inferences, this is done with a great deal of caution. Consent, even if inferred, must be *clearly present* and cannot be a mere technical creation or fiction by the Court.[36] This kind of approach ensures that the Court respects the principle of consent—that it must be clear, voluntary and indisputable.[37]

The principle of *Forum Prorogatum* pertains to the consent of a state to the court's jurisdiction, with reference to acts subsequent to the initial proceedings. This principle is set out in Article 38 (5). This is normally thought of as a two-step process: wherein the filing of an application by one state, is followed by an expression of consent to jurisdiction by the other state.[38] It usually arises when one party files an application with the Court, unilaterally inviting another state to accept jurisdiction regarding the dispute, where such jurisdiction would not otherwise exist with regard to the matter before it. If the other state accedes to this, then the Court will have jurisdiction in the matter.

The importance of the principle of consent in relation to third parties was mentioned in the case of *Cameroon v. Nigeria*,[39] where the ICJ stated that it would not entertain actions between states that implied a third state without its consent.[40] This refrain from bringing in third parties has been termed in international law as the 'indispensable third party principle'.[41] Furthermore, in Article 36 (6) of the Statute, it has been stated that the Court has the competence to decide its own jurisdiction in the event of a dispute.[42] Article 36 (2) provides an optional clause extending the jurisdiction of the International Court. This article is of immense importance and has often been called the 'optional clause' providing the option to significantly extend the Court's jurisdiction.[43] Parties to the present Statute can at any time declare that they recognise as compulsory *ipso facto* and without special agreement—in relation to any other state accepting the same obligation—the jurisdiction of the Court in all legal disputes concerning:

a) the interpretation of a treaty
b) any question of international law
c) the existence of any fact which, if established, would constitute a breach of an international obligation
d) the nature or extent of the reparation to be made for a breach of an international obligation.[44]

As Shaw notes, this provision was intended to operate as a method of increasing the Court's jurisdiction, through an increase in its acceptance by more and more states.[45] By the end of 1984, forty-seven declarations were in force and deposited with the UN Secretary General, comprising fewer than one-third of the parties to the ICJ Statute. By June 2020, this number had risen to seventy-four.[46] The day that one of those states accepts an offer by depositing in its turn the declaration of acceptance, the consensual bond is established, and no further obligation needs to be met.[47]

It is also important to emphasise that reciprocal declarations of two parties on the same issue or issues are not declarations of identical terms. The principle of time *ratione temporis* in the UN Secretary General's office is elaborated further, as some states exclude the jurisdiction of the ICJ with respect to disputes arising before or after a certain date in their declarations. The Court has reiterated there is a fundamental distinction between the existence of the Court's jurisdiction over a dispute, and the compatibility with international law of the acts which are subject of the dispute.[48]

The ICJ adopts the approach of observing equitable considerations within the framework of international law. This can be seen when the Court decided on the topic of self-defence. In the Advisory Opinion, *The Legality of the Threat or Use of Nuclear-Weapons*,[49] the Court took the view that it could not "conclude" definitively whether the threat or use of nuclear weapons would be lawful or unlawful in an extreme circumstance of self-defence, in which the very survival of a state would be at stake.[50]

Evidence

Now that we have some idea about the issue of jurisdiction under the ICJ, we can proceed to discuss the Court's position on evidence. Unlike domestic courts, the International Court is flexible regarding the introduction of evidence and does not have evidentiary rules that are as strict as most of its domestic counterparts.[51] The Court has the competence, *inter alia*, to determine the existence of any fact which, if established, would constitute a breach of an international obligation. In the *Genocide Convention (Bosnia v Serbia)* case, the Court emphasised that it had long recognised that "claims against a state involving charges of exceptional gravity must be proved by evidence that is fully conclusive."[52]

Based on Article 48 of the Statute, the Court has the authority to join cases into a single proceeding where the same overall situation is in evidence but this is rare. It can make all arrangements with regard to the taking and collection of evidence.[53] With reference to counter claims, the Court has directed that a party can introduce a new claim, provided that the additional claim is implicit in the application, or it must arise directly out of the question which is the subject matter of the application.[54]

Remedies

If an applicant state makes a declaratory judgement stating that the respondent has breached international law, such declarations may extend to provisions of future conduct as well as characterisation of past conduct. Requests for declaratory judgements may also be coupled with a request for reparation for losses suffered because of illegal activities, or damages for inquiry of various kinds, including non-material damage. In the *I'm Alone* case, the request was not only for direct injury to the state in question, but also with reference to its citizens or their property.[55]

In terms of principles of enforcement, Article 60 stipulates that the judgement of the court is final without appeal. Furthermore, Article 61 of the Statute stipulates that an application for revision of a judgement may only be made upon the discovery of a decisive fact which was, when the judgement was given, unknown to the Court and to the party claiming revision—provided that any ignorance was not due to negligence.[56] Application must be submitted no later than six months from the discovery of a new fact and ten years from the date of judgement.

Advisory Jurisdiction of the Court

Article 65 of the Statute declares that "the Court may give any advisory opinion on any legal question at the request of whatever body may be authorised by or in accordance with the Charter of the United Nations to make such a request." Article 96 of the Charter notes that as well as the General Assembly and Security Council, other organs of the UN and specialised agencies, where so authorised by the Assembly, may request such opinions on legal questions arising within the scope of their activities, and offer legal advice to those organs and institutions requesting the opinion.[57]

With regard to the Court's jurisdiction in providing opinions, Article 96 (2) of the Charter provides that, in addition to the Security Council and General Assembly:

> "[O]ther organs of the United Nations and specialised agencies which may at any time be so authorised by the General Assembly, may also request advisory opinions of the Court on legal questions arising within the scope of their activities."[58]

Conciliation

The process of conciliation involves a third-party investigation of the basis of the dispute, and the submission of a report proposing suggestions for a settlement.[59] As such, it involves elements of both inquiry and mediation, and in fact the process of conciliation emerged from treaties providing for permanent inquiry commissions.[60]

Conciliation reports are only proposals and, as such, do not constitute binding decisions.[61] They are thus different from arbitration awards that are binding and which were used more widely in the period between the world wars. "Nevertheless", Shaw notes, "conciliation processes do have a role to play. They are extremely flexible and, by clarifying the facts and discussing proposals, may stimulate negotiations between the parties."[62]

Article 15 (1) of the Geneva General Act, as amended, provides that:

> "The task of the Conciliation Commission shall be to elucidate the questions in dispute, to collect with that object all necessary information by means of enquiry or otherwise, and to endeavour to bring the parties to an agreement. It may, after the case has been examined, inform the parties of the term of settlement which seems suitable to it, and lay down the period within which they are to make their decision."[63]

There are many multi-lateral treaties that provide reconciliation as a means of resolving disputes. The 1948 American Treaty of Pacific Settlement; The 1957 European Convention for the Peaceful Settlement of Disputes; the 1964 Protocol on the Commission of Mediation; the 1969 Vienna Convention on the Law of Treaties; the 1975 Convention on the Representation of States in relation with International Organisations; the 1978 Vienna Convention on the Succession of States in respect of Treaties; the 1982 Convention on the Law of the Sea—and even the 1985 Vienna Convention on the Protection of the Ozone Layer—are all examples of this phenomena.[64]

In sum, the conciliation process's flexibility and unique way of facilitating dispute settlement is an important mechanism under international law.

International Institution Dispute Settlement

Regarding regional organisation, Article 52 (1) of Chapter VIII of the UN Charter provides that nothing in the Charter precludes the existence of regional arrangements or agencies for dealing with such matters relating to the maintenance of international peace and security, as are appropriate for regional action, provided that such arrangements or agencies and their activities are consistent with the purposes and principles of the UN.[65]

Article 52 (2) stipulates that member of the UN entering such arrangements or agencies are to make every effort to settle local disputes peacefully through such regional agencies, before referring them to the Security Council, and that the Security Council encourages the development of the peaceful settlement of local disputes through such regional arrangements. Article 52 (4) stresses that the application of Articles 34 and 35 of the UN Charter relating to the roles of the Security Council and General Assembly remains unaffected. Furthermore, Article 53 (1) stipulates that no enforcement action can commence without the authority of the Security Council.[66] In recent years, there has been a proliferation of Courts and Tribunals in international law at both an international and regional level. This development is reflected in the increasing scope and utilisation of international law, on the one hand, and the increasing emphasis on the value of resolving disputes by impartial third-party mechanisms, on the other. Shaw highlights the development of referral to courts and tribunals as an "an accepted international practice" for settling differences in a manner that is reflective of the rule of law and the growth of international cooperation.[67]

The developments described above further reinforce the importance of international law in an era of globalisation. There is also a range of regional organisations and forums that can be considered, when resolving disputes based on international law. These include the African Union, the ECOWAS, SADC, the Arab League, The European Convention for the Peaceful Settlement of Disputes, among others.

Use of Force

Article 2 (4) of the United Nations Charter urges that all members refrain in their international relations from the threat or use of force against the territorial integrity or political independence of any state, or in any other manner inconsistent with the purpose of the UN.[68] The provision—which is deeply significant in international law and polity—is worded as follows:

All Members shall refrain in their international relations from the threat or use of force against the territorial integrity or political independence of any state, or in any other manner inconsistent with the Purposes of the United Nations.[69]

The 1965 *Declaration on the Inadmissibility of Intervention in the Domestic Affairs of States* stipulates that no state has the right to intervene, directly or indirectly, regardless of the reason, in the internal or external affairs of any other state.[70] Subsequently, armed intervention and all other forms of interference, or attempted threats against the personality of the state or against its political, economic, and cultural elements, are condemned. This was reaffirmed in the 1970 *Declaration on Principles in International Law*, with the proviso that not only are such manifestations condemned, but they were also held to be in violation of international law.[71] The nucleus of these conclusions lay in the mutual respect by independent states of each other's territorial sovereignty.[72] There are numerous measures of self-help, ranging from economic retaliation to the use of violence, pursuant to the rights of self-defence that have historically been used. However, since the establishment of the charter, three classifications of compulsion are open to states under international law: retorsion, reprisal, and self-defence.

The Right of Self Defence: Article 51

The conventional definition of the right of self-defence in customary international law emanated out of the *Caroline* case.[73] Furthermore, in the *Nicaragua* case, the Court stated that this right of self-defence existed as an inherent right under customary international law as well as under the UN Charter.[74] The UN Secretary of State stated that the essentials of self-defence need to be "overwhelming, leaving no choice of means and no moment for deliberation."[75] The conditions of self-defence are legitimate, but the action taken in pursuance of it must not be unreasonable or excessive, "since the act, justified by the necessity of self-defence, must be limited by that necessity, and kept clearly within it."[76] There is thus a prevalent understanding that while self-defence is legitimate, it must be balanced by notions of proportionality or necessity: the action performed in self-defence must not be an *excessive use of force*. Indeed, the concepts of necessity and proportionality are central to the law on self-defence in international law.[77]

It is also important to consider the question of armed attacks and self-defence by non-state actors. While the notions of self-defence were normally or historically restricted to state actors, this cannot be read to mean that self-defence does not exist where there is an attack by a non-state entity emanating from a territory outside the control of the target state.[78] Another area to explore in this arena is the concept of anticipatory self-defence linked to modern warfare, drone, and nuclear attacks. An example of the principle of state anticipatory self-defence is provided by Israel's strike on its Arab neighbours in 1967. In contrast, preventive self-defence is based on the use of force to prevent a possible attack, or to engage in armed action to deter an avoidable attack. With regard to the US action in Afghanistan in 2001, the US to the UN on 7 October 2001 stated "we may find that our self-defence requires further actions with respect to other organisations and other states."[79] The 2002 National Security Strategy of the U.S.,[80] which was reaffirmed in the 2006 National Security Strategy, emphasised the role of pre-emption.[81] Shaw reiterates that "In so far as it goes beyond the Caroline Criteria, this doctrine of pre-emption must be seen as going beyond what is currently acceptable in international law."[82]

Another important principle in international humanitarian law is that of reprisals and the principle of proportionality. In *the Legality of the Threat or Use of Nuclear Weapons* case, the International Court took the view that the proportionality principle may "not in itself exclude the use of nuclear weapons in self-defence in all circumstances;" but that "a use of force that is proportionate under the law of self-defence, must, in order to be lawful, also meet the requirements of the law applicable in armed conflict."[83] In practice, we can understand this principle better through illustrations. Consider the case of the US and its intervention in Iraq. In 2020, the US President Donald Trump ordered a drone strike that killed Iranian Military Commander Qasem Soleimani in Iraq and exclaimed that it was undertaken to "deter future Iranian attack plans."[84] A 2010 UN report on "targeted killings" said there was a weighty body of scholarship that viewed the self-defence argument as having the right to use force "against a real and imminent threat when the necessity of that self-defence is instant, overwhelming, and leaving no choice of means, and no moment of deliberation."[85] The initial US Department of Defence statement omitted the word "imminent",[86] and said that the strike was aimed at deterring future Iranian attacks and that Iran's top military leader Soleimani was "actively developing plans to attack American diplomats and service members in Iraq and throughout the region." In later statements, US officials, including President Trump, said Soleimani had been plotting "imminent attacks."[87]

In this case, many proponents of international law felt that the test of anticipatory self-defence had not been met by the USA in this scenario.[88] There was also a feeling that, in this situation, the US had not sought the consent of Iraq to carry out the drone strike, and deemed it a "brazen violation of Iraq's sovereignty."[89]

In addition, in other instances we can see that, for states to force to repeal an attack, such as in the *Falklands Conflict*, it was clear that after the Argentinian invasion of the territory, the United Kingdom possessed, in law, the right to act to restore the status quo ante and remove the Argentinian troops.[90] These illustrations help clarify the stance on armed self-defence.

Another important principle in international humanitarian law is that of collective self-defence. While the right of state to take up arms in self-defence is an established rule in international law, Article 51 also interestingly mentions the "inherent right of ... collective self-defence".[91] There is much to be discussed regarding this collective right. Principally, would we consider it to be a collection or merely a "pooling" of several individual rights? Or rather, is there something else to the collective that cannot be thought of merely as a sum of its constituent parts? Shaw notes that if an approach closer to the latter is taken, it can pave the way for "comprehensive regional security systems".[92] This is an area of emerging interest for scholars and practitioners in the field of international law.

Civil Wars

International law treats civil wars essentially as internal matters for states to deal with—with the possible exception of self-determination conflicts.[93] Article 2 (4) of the UN Charter[94] prohibits the threat or use of force in international relations, in domestic situations. There is, however, no rule against rebellion in international law.[95] The domestic jurisdiction of states is left to be addressed by internal law. For third parties, traditional international law developed the categories of rebellion, insurgency, and belligerency. Humanitarian interventions that are carried out under the pretext to protect the lives of certain persons situated within a particular state—and not necessarily nationals of the intervening state—are permissible in strictly defined situations. However, this is difficult to reconcile with

Article 2 (4), which permits temporary violations of the right of customary law.

The Kosovo Crisis of 1999 firmly raised the issue of intervention in order to avoid a humanitarian catastrophe. The operation to evacuate British nationals and eligible Afghans from Afghanistan in 2021, Operating Pitting, can also be deemed an example of this. McKinley's *Foreign Policy* piece titled "Afghanistan's Looming Catastrophe" raises serious concerns, however, about the post-withdrawal situation that has unfolded in Afghanistan and advocates certain reforms of international law to prevent a humanitarian catastrophe from unfolding.[96]

The situation in Afghanistan raises another key principle in international law, that of the "responsibility to protect", which includes the obligation to prevent catastrophic situations and to react immediately when they do occur and to rebuild thereafter.[97] A further critical area of importance is that of terrorism and international law, along with its interaction with principles of human rights. Progress has been made on the rules in international law regarding terrorism, but the definition of terrorism in customary international law is a matter of some controversy. The UN has attempted to address the question of terrorism in a comprehensive fashion. In December 1972, the General Assembly set up an ad hoc committee on terrorism,[98] and in 1994 a Declaration on Measures to Eliminate International Terrorism was adopted. There are thus a range of regional instruments that are used to suppress terrorism.[99]

International Humanitarian Law

As with the subject of the laws of war, armed conflict tends to be looked at within the rubric of international humanitarian law. It is primarily derived from international conventions and some customary international law. It is feasible to say that several customary international law principles exist over and above conventional rules, albeit international humanitarian law is one of the most highly codified parts of international law.

There has been an alignment of international humanitarian law, human rights, and criminal law. The laws of war were codified at the Hague Conferences of 1899 and 1907. The Four Geneva "Red Cross" Conventions of 1949 dealt respectively with the care of wounded, sick and shipwrecked members of the armed forces at sea, the treatment of prisoners of war, and the protection of civilian persons in time of war. The Fourth Convention was an innovative step, and a significant attempt to protect civilians who, because of armed hostilities or occupation, were under the power of a state of which they were not nationals. Owing to the influence of human rights law and relevant domestic provisions, this offshoot of the law is increasingly complex and sophisticated.

International humanitarian law also deals with the situation of combatants and non-combatants. Common Article 2 of the Geneva Convention provides that the Convention:

> Shall apply to all cases of declared war or of any other armed conflict which may arise between two or more of the High Contracting Parties even if the state of war is not recognised by them and to all cases of partial or total occupation of the territory of a High Contracting Party, even if the said occupation meets with no armed resistance.[100]

The rules cited in these Conventions cannot be reneged by those intended to benefit from them, thus precluding the likelihood that the power which has control over them may seek to influence the persons concerned to agree a mitigation of protection.

The scope and protection under international humanitarian law include the wounded and sick. The First Geneva Convention concerns the wounded and sick on land, along with members of the armed forces and organised militias, including those duly accompanying them, are to be respected and protected in all circumstances."[101] The Second Geneva Convention, addressing "Wounded, Sick, and Shipwrecked Members of the Armed Forces at Sea" is similar to the first convention. The Third Geneva Convention of 1949 address the positions of prisoners of war. It consists of a comprehensive code centred upon the requirement for humane treatment in all circumstances. The definition of prisoners of war in Article 4, however, is of particular importance since it has been regarded as an elaboration of combatant status. Articles 43 and 44 of Protocol I, 1977 state that combatants are members of the armed forces of a party to an international armed conflict.[102] Article 13 stipulates that prisoner of war are to be treated humanely, protected against acts of violence, intimidation, and against "insults and public curiosity." Displaying prisoners of war on TV (for instance) in a humiliating fashion is considered to be a breach of the convention. Measures of reprisal against prisoners of war are also prohibited. Article 14 provides that prisoners of war are entitled in all circumstances to respect of their persons and their honour.[103]

The Convention on prisoners of war applies only to international armed conflicts, but Article 3, which is common to the four conventions, provides that, as a minimum, "persons taking no active part in the hostilities, including members of the armed forces, who have laid down their arms and those placed *hors de combat* by sickness, wounds, detention, and any other cause, shall in all circumstance be treated humanely, without any adverse distinction founded on race, colour, religion or faith, sex, birth or wealth, or any other similar criteria."[104]

The Fourth Geneva Convention focuses on the protection of civilians in time of war, and builds on the *Hague Regulations*, which are attached to the *Hague Convention IV on the Law and Custom of War on Land, 1907*.[105] With reference to the military occupation of enemy territory, international law establishes a legal framework concerning the appropriate legal positions of occupier and occupied.

International human rights law can be seen, in principle, to apply to occupation situations. Article 43 of the *Hague Regulations*[106] places a duty to secure respects for the applicable rules of international human rights law and international humanitarian law, to protect the inhabitants of the occupied territory against acts of violence, and not to tolerate such violence by any third-party state.

The Court has noted that the principle of self-determination applies to the Palestinian people,[107] and that the construction by Israel of a separation barrier (sometimes termed a wall or a fence) between its territory and the occupied West Bank was unlawful to the extent that it was situated within the occupied territories. Although an occupying power can plead military exigencies and the requirements of national security or public order within the framework of the international law of occupation, the route of the wall could not be justified as the international convention on human rights applied in this area.

Article 4 of the Right to Life of the *African Charter on Human and Peoples' Rights* notes:

> In armed conflict, what constitutes an "arbitrary" deprivation of life during the conduct of hostilities is to be determined by reference to International Humanitarian Law. This law does not prohibit the use of force in hostilities against lawful targets (for example combatants or civilians directly participating in hostilities) if necessary, from a military perspective, provided that, in all circumstances, the rules of distinction, proportionality and precaution in attack are observed. Any violation of International Humanitarian Law resulting in death, including war crimes, will be an arbitrary deprivation of life.[108]

International humanitarian law also includes provisions on detention and prisoners of war.[109] In the case of *Croatia v Serbia*, the ICJ ruled that whilst it could not rule out the relationship between the Genocide Convention and international humanitarian law,[110] the rules of international humanitarian law may be of relevance to decide whether the alleged acts of parties constitute genocide within the meaning of Article II of the Genocide Convention.[111]

Although reprisals utilising the use of force are now prohibited in international law (unless they can be justified within the framework of self-defence) belligerent reprisals during an armed conflict may, in certain circumstances, be legitimate. Their purpose is to ensure the termination of the prior unlawful act which precipitated the initial reprisal and facilitate a return to legality. It is imperative that the reprisal is proportionate to the prior illegal act.[112] The ICJ has stated that at the heart of international customary law is the "overriding consideration of humanity", irrespective of whether states had ratified the Geneva Convention.[113]

Nuclear Weapons

The possession and threat of nuclear weapons is controversial in international humanitarian law. The International Court has emphasised that, in examining the legality of any situation, the principles regulating the resort to force, including the right to self-defence, need to be coupled with the additional requirement to consider the norms governing the means and methods of warfare itself.

Accordingly, the types of weapons used, and the ways in which they are used, are also part of the legal equation in analysing the legitimacy of any use of force in international law. The Court analysed state practices and concluded that nuclear weapons were not prohibited either specifically or by express provision;[114] nor were they prohibited by analogy with poisoned gases, prohibited under the *Second Hague Declaration* of 1899, Article 23(a) of the *Hague Regulations* of 1907, and the *Geneva Protocol* of 1925.[115] They were neither prohibited by the series of treaties[116] concerning the acquisition, manufacture, deployment and testing of nuclear weapons, and the treaties concerning the ban on such weapons in certain areas of the world. Nor are they prohibited by General Assembly resolutions which as a collective fell short in creating a new rule to this affect. [117]

With reference to the principles of international humanitarian law, the Court, beyond noting their applicability, could not reach a conclusion. The Court was unable to determine whether the principle of neutrality, the principles of international humanitarian law, or, indeed, the norm of self-defence, prohibited the threat or use of nuclear weapons.[118] In 1995, five nuclear weapon states announced that they would not use such weapons against non-nuclear weapons states that are parties to the *Nuclear Non-Proliferation Treaty*.[119]

Another issue relevant in the realm of international humanitarian law is the use of drones. Whilst their utilisation is not illegal per se, their use is regulated via the same rules as those that pertain to manual aircraft, and general humanitarian law.[120]

Armed Conflicts- International and Internal Dimensions

The rules of international humanitarian law apply to armed conflict. There is no formal announcement of war that is required for the Conventions to apply. It is noted that any difference arising between states that leads to the intervention of members of the armed forces is an "armed conflict", and "an armed conflict" exists whenever there is a resort to armed force between states or protracted armed violence between governmental authorities and organised armed groups within a state.[121]

There is also the realm of non-international armed conflict, as well as mixed international Conflicts. In its decision on jurisdictional issues in the *Tadic* case, the Appeals Chamber of the International Criminal Tribunal for the Former Yugoslavia attempted to make the argument that no conflict existed in the former Yugoslavia, as the concept of armed conflict covered only the precise time and place of the actual hostilities. The Appeal Chamber refused such a narrow definition and stated:

> International Humanitarian Law applies from the initiation of such armed conflicts and extends beyond the cessation of hostilities until a general conclusion of peace is reached; or, in the case of internal conflicts, a peaceful settlement is achieved. Until that moment, International Humanitarian Law continues to apply in the whole territory of the warring state or, in the case of internal conflicts, the whole territory under the control of the party, whether or not actual combat takes place.[122]

The above decision is of crucial importance in clarifying the applicable law and its application to conflict situations. The Security Council Resolution 771 (1992) did not, as such, classify the nature of the conflict; it simply called for its cessation and condemned widespread violations of international humanitarian law and, subsequently, the Appeal Chamber concluded that conflicts in the former Yugoslavia have both internal and international aspects.[123]

Conflict can assume an international dimension depending on the circumstances. It can also be international in character alongside an internal armed conflict, if another state intervenes in that conflict through its troops, or, alternatively, if some of the participants in the internal armed conflict act on behalf of another state. Although the 1949 Geneva Conventions were concerned with international armed conflicts, common Article 3[124] did provide minimum guarantees for non-combatants in cases of non-international armed conflicts occurring in the territory of one of the parties. These guarantees included the sick and wounded. The Court in the Nicaragua case[125] declared that common Article 3 also applied to international armed conflicts as a "minimum yardstick, in addition to the more elaborate rules which are also to apply to international conflicts."[126]

International Human Rights Law

The distinction between inter-state and civil wars was losing its value as far as human beings were concerned. There has been a fundamental shift in human rights law, founded on the principle of the respect for human dignity.

The governing principles regarding internal armed conflicts in humanitarian law are becoming more extensive, while the principles of international human rights law are also rapidly evolving—particularly with reference to fundamental non-derogable rights which cannot be breached even in times of public emergency.[127] These fundamental rights can be found in Article 15 of ECHR, 1950; Article 4 of the *International Covenant on Civil and Political Rights*, 1966;[128] and Article 27 of the *Inter-American Convention on Human Rights*, 1969.[129]

A set of minimum humanitarian standards was adopted by the International Committee of the Red Cross in 1990.[130] The declaration emphasises the prohibition against violence with regard to life, health and physical and mental well-being of persons, including murder, torture and rape; collective punishment; hostage-taking; practising, permitting, or tolerating the involuntary disappearance of individuals; pillage; deliberate deprivation of access to necessary food, drinking of water and medicine; and threats or incitement to commit any of these acts.[131]

The ICRC has set out seven high level principles as a guide to the legal rules that states need to observe, as part of international humanitarian law, when engaged in conflicts.[132] They differentiate between civilian and military targets, and attacks directed solely against military objectives. The relevant legal rules set a barometer to judge the actions of states, and especially as to whether they are meeting the principles and standards of international humanitarian law.

What resides at the core of the coverage of international law on the topics of conflict resolution, arbitration, and peacekeeping is that of the protection and preservation of humanity. This is critical in the discourse of international law.

Thus far, we have now an idea about the framework of international law regarding the settlement of disputes. This overview has helped uncover the many core questions at stake in our discussions on dispute settlement and demonstrated the various mechanisms available to states under international law. We are now well-placed to begin our comparative endeavour—and ask how the core principles of Islamic Law and Jurisprudence can inform these debates.

References

Art 43-Armed Forces, IHL Treaties – Additional Protocol (I) to the Geneva Conventions, 1977 – Article 43 (icrc.org) (Accessed January 3, 2022).

Convention (IV) respecting the Laws and Customs of War on Land and its annex: Regulations concerning the Laws and Customs of War on Land. The Hague, 18 October 1907. IHL Treaties - Hague Convention (IV) on War on Land and its Annexed Regulations, 1907 (icrc.org) (Accessed January 1, 2022).

Article 44-Combatants and Prisoner of War, Geneva Conventions of 1949, Additional Protocols and their Commentaries: - IHL Treaties - Additional Protocol (I) to the Geneva Conventions, 1977 - Article 44 (icrc.org) (Accessed January 3, 2022).

1899 Hague Convention for the Pacific Settlement of International Disputes, available online at: https://docs.pca-cpa.org/2016/01/1899-Convention-for-the-Pacific-Settlement-of-International-Disputes.pdf (Accessed 3rd January, 2022)

Art.43 Hague Regulations: IHL Treaties - Hague Convention (II) on the Laws and Customs of War on Land, 1899 - Regulations: Art. 43 (icrc.org) (Accessed January 1, 2022).

Convention (I) for the Amelioration of the Condition of the Wounded and Sick in Armed Forces in the Field, Geneva, 12 August 1949. IHL Treaties - Geneva Convention (I) on Wounded and Sick in Armed Forces in the Field,1949 (icrc.org), (Accessed January 3, 2022)

ICRC Commentary on the First Geneva Convention published online in March 2016, IHL Treaties - Geneva Convention (I) on Wounded and Sick in Armed Forces in the Field,1949 - Commentary of 2016 Foreword | Foreword | Foreword (icrc.org) (Accessed January 3, 2022).

Charter of the United Nations, 1945, United Nations Charter (full text) | United Nations (Accessed 31 December 2021)

Daniel Webster, *Letter from U.S. Secretary of State Daniel Webster to British Minister Henry Fox* (24 April 1841), 29 BRrr. & FOR. ST. PAPERS 1137 (1841).

Evans G., et al, *The Responsibility to Protect. Report of the International Commission on Intervention and State Sovereignty*. Ottawa: International Development Research Centre, 2001. Available online at: https://undocs.org/pdf?symbol=en/a/57/303 (Accessed 3rd January, 2022)

General Assembly Resolution 43/51, *Declaration on the Prevention and Removal of Disputes and Situations Which May Threaten International Peace and Security and on the Role of the United Nations in This Field* (5 December 1988) UN Doc A/RES/43/51. Available online at: https://www.refworld.org/docid/3b00f2274b.html (Accessed 3rd March, 2022)

General Assembly Resolution 2131 (XX), *Declaration on the Inadmissibility of Intervention in the Domestic Affairs of States and the Protection of Their Independence and Sovereignty* (21 December 1965). Available online at: http://www.worldlii.org/int/other/UNGA/1965/124.pdf (Accessed 3rd March, 2022)

General Assembly Resolution 2626 (XXV), *Declaration on Principles of International Law concerning Friendly Relations and Cooperation among States in accordance with the Charter of the United Nations* (24 October 1970) UN Doc A/RES/2625(XXV). Available online at: https://digitallibrary.un.org/record/202170?ln=en (Accessed 3rd March, 2022)

General Assembly Resolution 3034, *Measures to Prevent International Terrorism* (18 December 1972) UN Doc A/RES/3034 (XXVII). Available online at: https://unispal.un.org/DPA/DPR/unispal.nsf/85255db800470aa485255d8b004e349a/69cb600fbde9eddd852570840050c345?OpenDocument (Accessed 3rd March, 2022)

General Assembly Resolution 3314 (XXIX), *Definition of Aggression* (14 December 1974). Available online at: https://legal.un.org/avl/pdf/ha/da/da_e.pdf (Accessed 3rd March, 2022)

General Assembly, *A More Secure World: Our Shared Responsibility. Report of the High-Level Panel on Threats, Challenges, and Change* (2 December 2004) UN Doc A/59/565. Available online at: https://www2.ohchr.org/english/bodies/hrcouncil/docs/gaA.59.565_En.pdf (Accessed 3rd March, 2022)

General Assembly, *In Larger Freedom: Towards Development, Security, and Human Rights for All, Report of the Secretary General* (26 May 2005) UN Doc A/59/2005/Add.3. Available online at: https://www.ohchr.org/Documents/Publications/A.59.2005.Add.3.pdf (Accessed 3rd March, 2022)

Art 15(1) of *1928 General Act on the Pacific Settlement of International Disputes* (revised in 1949). 1928-General-Act-of-Arbitration.pdf (nus.edu.sg) (Accessed 31 December 2021).

Art 3 and 4, Geneva Convention Relative to the Treatment of Prisoners of War, 12 August 1949, Geneva Convention relative to the Treatment of Prisoners of War | OHCHR (Accessed January 1, 2022).

Goodman, R. "Authorization versus Regulation of Detention in Non-International Armed Conflicts." *International Law Studies* 91 (2015): 155–70. (Accessed 4th March, 2022)

Gray, C. "The Bush Doctrine Revisited: The 2006 National Security Strategy of the USA." *Chinese Journal of International Law* 5/3 (2006): 555–78.

Hassan v. The United Kingdom, European Court of Human Rights, Grand Chamber, Application no. 29750/09, Judgment, Strasbourg, 16 September 2014. Available online at http://hudoc.echr.coe.int/sites/eng (Accessed 4th March, 2022)

International Committee of the Red Cross (ICRC), *Article 2: Application of the Convention*. Available online at: https://ihl-databases.icrc.org/applic/ihl/ihl.nsf/Comment.xsp?action=openDocument&documentId=BE2D518CF5DE54EAC1257F7D0036B518 (Accessed 4th March, 2022)

International Committee of the Red Cross (ICRC), *Geneva Convention Relative to the Protection of Civilian Persons in Time of War (Fourth Geneva Convention)* 75 UNTS 287 (12 August 1949). Available online at https://www.refworld.org/docid/3ae6b36d2.html (Accessed 4th March, 2022)

International Committee of the Red Cross (ICRC), *Report of the International Committee of the Red Cross (ICRC) on the Treatment by the Coalition Forces of Prisoners of War and Other Protected Persons by the Geneva Conventions in Iraq during Arrest, Internment, and Interrogation* (2004). Available online at https://cryptome.org/icrc-report.htm (Accessed 5th March, 2022)

International Committee of the Red Cross (ICRC), *International Review of the Red Cross* 272 (Sept.–Oct. 1989). Available online at: https://international-review.icrc.org/reviews/irrc-no-272-international-review-red-cross-10-1989 (Accessed 5th March, 2022)

International Court of Justice Annual Reports. Available online at https://www.icj-cij.org/en/annual-reports (Accessed 5th March, 2022)

Art 96(2), Chapter XIV- The International Court of Justice, Charter of the United Nations, 1945. Chapter XIV: Article 96 — Charter of the United Nations — Repertory of Practice of United Nations Organs — Codification Division Publications (Accessed 31 December 2021).

International Court of Justice, Legal Consequences of the Construction of a Wall in the Occupied Palestinian Territory Advisory Opinion No. 2004/28, 9 July 2004, 131-20040709-PRE-01-00-EN.pdf (icj-cij.org) (Accessed January 1, 2022).

Jonkman, H. "The Role of the Permanent Court of Arbitration in International Dispute Resolution." 279 *Receuil des cours* (1999): 9–49. (Accessed 5th March, 2022)

Lauterpacht, H. *The Function of Law in the International Community*. London: Garland, 1933.

Letter dated 95/01/05 from the Permanent Representative of Norway and the Chargé d'Affaires of the Permanent Mission of Finland addressed to the Commission on Human Rights, E/CN.4/1995/116 (1995). Available online at https://digitallibrary.un.org/record/226914?ln=en (Accessed 5th March, 2022)

Manila Declaration on the Peaceful Settlement of International Disputes (15 November 1982). Available online at: https://cil.nus.edu.sg/wp-content/uploads/formidable/18/1982-Manila-Declaration-on-the-Peaceful-Settlement-of-International-Disputes.pdf (Accessed 5th March, 2022)

Mavrommatis Palestine Concessions (Greece v. U.K.), 1924 P.C.I.J. (ser. B) No. 3 (Aug. 30). Available online at: http://www.worldcourts.com/pcij/eng/decisions/1924.08.30_mavrommatis.htm (Accessed 5th March, 2022)

McKinley, P. M. "Afghanistan's Looming Catastrophe." *Foreign Affairs* (December 3, 2021). Available online at https://www.foreignaffairs.com/articles/afghanistan/2021-12-03/afghanistans-looming-catastrophe (Accessed 5th March, 2022)

Meron, T. and Rosas, A. "A Declaration of Minimum Humanitarian Standards." *American Journal of International Law* 85/2 (2017): 375–81.
M. Hosenball, Trump says Soleimani plotted 'imminent' attacks, but critics question just how soon | Reuters, Jan 3, 2020. (Accessed 5th March, 2022)

Office of the High Commissioner for Human Rights, *Minimum Humanitarian Standards*, E/CN.4/RES/1995/29. Available online at: https://ap.ohchr.org/documents/alldocs.aspx?doc_id=4304 (Accessed 5th March, 2022)

Organization for Security and Co-operation in Europe, *Action Against Terrorism*. Available online at: www.osce.org/secretariat/terrorism (Accessed 6th March, 2022)

Reality Check Team (BBC News), "Soleimani Attack: What does International Law Say?" BBC News, January 7, 2020. Available online at https://www.bbc.com/news/world-51007961 (Accessed 5th March, 2022)

Shahabuddeen, M. *Precedent in the World Court*. Cambridge: Cambridge University Press, 1996.

Shaw, M. N. *International Law*, 8th edn. Cambridge: Cambridge University Press, 2017.
Art.2, Statute of the International Court of Justice, 1945, Statute of the Court | International Court of Justice (icj-cij.org), (Accessed 30 January, 2022).

Art 36 (2), *Statute of The International Court of Justice*, 1945, Statute of the Court | International Court of Justice (icj-cij.org) (Accessed 30 January, 2022).

Art 96(2), Chapter XIV- The International Court of Justice, Charter of the United Nations, 1945. Chapter XIV: Article 96 — Charter of the United Nations — Repertory of Practice of United Nations Organs — Codification Division Publications (Accessed 31 December 2021).

United Nations, *Treaty on the Non-Proliferation of Nuclear Weapons (NPT)*. Available online at: https://www.un.org/disarmament/wmd/nuclear/npt/text/" (Accessed 6th March, 2022)

United Nations Charter, Chapter VI: Pacific Settlement of Disputes, Art.33, 1945. Chapter VI: Pacific Settlement of Disputes (Articles 33-38) | United Nations (Accessed January 3, 2002).

United Nations, *Charter of the United Nations*, 1945. Available online at: https://www.un.org/en/about-us/un-charter/full-text (Accessed 6th March, 2022)

United Nations, *United Nations Convention on the Law of the Sea* (10 December 1982). Available online at:
https://www.un.org/depts/los/convention_agreements/texts/unclos/unclos_e.pdf"
https://www.un.org/depts/los/convention_agreements/texts/unclos/unclos_e.pdf (Accessed 6th March, 2022)

United Nations, *Vienna Convention on the Law of Treaties* (1969). Available online at:
https://legal.un.org/ilc/texts/instruments/english/conventions/1_1_1969.pdf. (Accessed 6th March, 2022)

United Nations, *Vienna Convention on the Representation of States in their Relations with International Organizations of a Universal Character* (1975). Available online at:
https://legal.un.org/ilc/texts/instruments/english/conventions/5_1_1975.pdf (Accessed 7th March, 2022)

United Nations Economic and Social Council, *Effective Functioning of Bodies Established Pursuant to United Nations Human Rights Instruments*, E/CN.4/1995/81. Available online at
https://documents-dds-ny.un.org/doc/UNDOC/GEN/G94/750/98/PDF/G9475098.pdf?OpenElement (Accessed 7th March, 2022)

United Nations Security Council, Resolution 502 (3 April 1982) UN Doc S/RES/502(1982). Available online at:
https://digitallibrary.un.org/record/34455?ln=en"
https://digitallibrary.un.org/record/34455?ln=en (Accessed 7th March, 2022)

United Nations Security Council, Resolution 984 (11 April 1995) UN Doc S/RES/984(1995). Available online at:
https://digitallibrary.un.org/record/176507?ln=en"
https://digitallibrary.un.org/record/176507?ln=en (Accessed 5th March, 2022)

United Nations Security Council, *Statute of the International Tribunal for Rwanda* (8 November 1994) UN Doc S/RES/955. Available online at: https://legal.un.org/avl/pdf/ha/ictr_ef.pdf (Accessed 7th March, 2022)

United Nations Security Council, S/2001/946. *Letter dated 7 October 2001 from the Permanent Representative of the United States of America to the United Nations addressed to the President of the Security Council.* 2001 Letter dated 7 October 2001 from the Permanent Representative of the United States of America to the United Nations addressed to the President of the Security Council (Accessed January 1, 2022).

Art.4 and Art. 27, United Nations International Covenant on Civil and Political Rights, 16 December 1966, General Assembly Resolution 2200A (XXI), International Covenant on Civil and Political Rights | OHCHR (Accessed January 3, 2022).

CHAPTER TWO

CONFLICT RESOLUTION, ARBITRATION, AND PEACEKEEPING/BUILDING BASED ON SOURCES OF ISLAMIC LAW

Abstract

If we venture outside the domain of international law, we see that there is in fact valuable material in other areas of legal thought. I draw from one such system of legal thought: Islamic law. I show that there is a wealth of material in Islamic Law that can add new and valuable perspectives to core issues in international law and policy—particularly on discourses about peacebuilding and the resolution of conflict.

This chapter will analyse the sources in Islamic Law that address the topic of Conflict Resolution, Arbitration, Peace and Reconciliation. It will also explore and analyse the modalities around Counter Terrorism, Sanctity, Safety, and Protection within the Islamic tradition, Islamic Human Rights Law and Diplomatic tools that are available in Islam to facilitate the pathways towards conflict resolution, peace and reconciliation between parties. Cumulatively, this chapter seeks to start a dialogue between Islamic law and international law—showing that material in the former can greatly influence core discussions in the latter.

The Concept of Peace in International Islamic Law

How does Islamic law construct the idea of 'peace'? What images of 'peace' do we find in this rich religious material? Before one embarks on describing the concept of peace or "peacebuilding",[133] it is important to clarify what is meant by "Shari'a" or "Islamic law." These terms are often used interchangeably in contemporary discourse, but they do, in fact, possess different connotations derived from the classical Islamic tradition. In the introductory chapter to his book *Reasoning with God*, Khaled Abou El Fadl provides a description of "Shari'a":

"In the linguistic practices of Islamic theologians, ethicists, and jurists in the Islamic tradition, the broad meaning of Shari'a is the way or path to well-being or goodness, the life source for wellbeing and thriving existence, the fountain or source of nourishment, and the natural and innate ways and order created by God." [134]

Shaheen Sardar Ali expounds on this further, stating, in essence, that Shari'a means "a flowing stream that brings nourishment, flourishing and life."[135] As to what constitutes "Islamic law", El Fadl describes it in the following terms:

The Islamic legal system consists of legal institutions, determinations, and practices that span a period of over fourteen hundred years, arising from a wide variety of cultural and geographic contexts that are as diverse as Arabia, Egypt, Persia, Bukhara, Turkey, Liberia, Nigeria, Mauritania, Mali, Indonesia, India and China.

He further asserts that the goal of Islamic law is to ensure human well-being (*tahqiq masalih al-'ibad*).[136] El Fadl adds that "Islamic law is best described as the process of a practiced discipline of deliberative and purposeful practical reasoning in which rulings are developed primarily through analogical dynamics."[137] It is this diversity and complexity of the divine indicators, as part of the Islamic jurisprudential model, that constitute the functionality and suitability of Islamic law for all times and places.[138]

The word "peace" in the classical Islamic tradition typifies a situation and state of tranquillity, harmony and balance between one's inner temporal self and one's fellow beings. It also is an embodiment and manifestation of a state of submission in the divine decree, where one is pleased with what the Lord has ordained for an individual and the Lord is also pleased (*nafs al mutmainah*),[139] this is a situation that is further personified in the exalted state and rank ascribed to the companions of the Prophet Muhammad.[140]

The root word for "peace" within the Islamic tradition is "*salaam.*" It has a multitude of meanings, ranging from "soundness, well-being, safety, security, general welfare, [and] intactness."[141] This image is further exemplified by what is commonly called the "*Darussalam*"—namely, "The House of Peace." It is also one of the Ninety-Nine Names of God, typifying that the source and manifestation of peace emanates from none other than the divine. Within the rubric of international Islamic law (*siyar*), peace is embedded at the heart of its tenets. The Qur'an also touches on the theme of peace when it states "… but if they incline to peace, you also incline to it."[142] We thus see that peace is a central idea in Islamic religious texts and practice.

The Concept of Reconciliation and Resolution in International Islamic Law

Moving now from the notion of 'peace' to the closely related idea of 'conflict reconciliation', it is important to note that the latter is also a crucial idea in Islamic law. The direction to strive towards promoting reconciliation amongst people can be found in the Qur'anic dictum:

> ...So, if a person fears any partiality by a testator (for someone) or injustice (towards some other), and then brings about reconciliation amongst them, it shall be no sin on him. Verily, God is Most Forgiving, Ever-Merciful. [143]

Reconciliation is thus thought of as being valuable within the tradition, and it must be strived for among people.

Islamic law also specifically discusses the resolution of conflict. There are numerous prophetic narrations that cover the resolution of interpersonal conflicts. An example is on the topic of charity, on which the Prophet Muhammad said:

> Charitable donation is incumbent every day on every joint of a human being on which the sun rises. It is charity to decide with justice between two people. Helping a person to mount a riding animal or putting their luggage over it is also almsgiving. Saying something good, every step taken towards offering the ritual prayer and clearing trouble from the road are also acts of charity (altruism).[144]

Islamic Legal Sources on Peace and Reconciliation

The direction to strive towards peace and reconciliation amongst people can be found in numerous Qur'anic dictums:

> And because of your oaths, do not use (the Name of) God as an excuse for refraining from doing good (to the people), becoming Godfearing and making peace amongst people. And God is All-Hearing, All-Knowing.[145]

In the following passage it is stipulated:

> There is no good in most of their secret consultations except (the counsel) of the person who enjoins charity or piety or peace-making amongst people. And whoever does this, seeking God's pleasure, we shall soon bless him with a mighty reward.[146]

And in another passage:

> And if two parties of the Muslims fight, make them reconcile. Then if either of these (parties) commits injustice and aggression against the other, fight

against (the party) that is committing the aggression till it return to God's command (of establishing peace). When they revert and submit, make peace between them with equity. And put justice to work. Surely, God loves those who do justice. The truth is that (all) believers are brothers (or sisters) (to one anotherr).[147] So, make peace between your two brothers (or sisters) and always fear God, so that you may be shown mercy.[148]

There are also many prophetic narrations advocating peace and reconciliation between parties. To cite a few examples:

The liar is not the one who reconciles the people (by lying). So, he/she relates and promotes something good (amongst the parties about one another for reconciliation).[149]

He who is allusive in bringing reconciliation between two people is not a liar.[150]

He is not a liar who brings reconciliation between two, saying something good (from his/her side) or attributing something good (to someone).[151]

The Prophet Muhammad also said: "The best charity is to bring reconciliation between two close relatives."[152] In another narration, according to Abu Umamah, the Prophet Muhammad said to Ayyub b. Zayd:

Shall I not inform you about an act that pleases God and His Prophet)? He submitted: "Why not, O Prophet of God!" He said: "When people fight, bring reconciliation amongst them and when distance occurs, create nearness amongst them."[153]

It is apparent that promoting peace and reconciliation is part of the core foundation stones of the Islamic tradition and legal structural norms.

A key component in conflict resolution is the ability to forgive. There are numerous Qur'anic dictums and prophetic narrations that highlight the strength and favour of the party *that is able to forgive*. An example is the prophetic statement reported by Aby Nu'aym:

According to Fudayl b. Iyad:

When someone complains to you about another person, say: "Whoever forgives and brings peace, his reward lies with God. And the bearer of forgiveness sleeps well in their bed at night while the dominant turns their matters topsy-turvy."[154]

The capacity to forgive is thus considered to be a virtue and facilitates conflict resolution, as constructed in Islamic law and theory.

Counter Terrorism within the Islamic Tradition

Furthermore, we can note that the unjust killing of another human being is categorically condemned in the Islamic tradition, as is the act of committing suicide. On the latter, the Qur'an stipulates:

> And do not kill yourselves. Surely, God is Kind to you. But whoever will do that through transgression and injustice, We shall soon throw him/her into the Fire (of Hell) and that is very easy for God.[155]

On the former, it stipulates:

> Whoever killed a person (unjustly), except as punishment for murder or for (spreading) disorder in the land, it would be as if he/she killed all the people (of society); and whoever (saved from unjust murder and) and made him/her survive, it would be as if he/she saved the lives of all the people (of society, i.e., he/she rescued the collective system of human life).[156]

The killing of one person unjustly is akin to killing all the people of society. This has also been affirmed by scholars of classical exegesis, such as Abu Hafs al-Hanbali[157] and al-Hasan al Basri.[158] These experts interpreted the same verse to imply that the perpetrator of the crime of killing is liable to legal retribution (*qisas*) for killing an innocent harmless soul, similar to the retribution applicable to one who has killed all of humanity. There is therefore the belief that the act of killing someone is not just a crime against that individual. Rather, the realm of the individual is transcended—and the images of wrongs against humanity seem to be invoked.

Furthermore, unjust and unlawful killing of innocence is reaffirmed by the following Qur'anic verse:

> And do not kill any soul whose (killing) God has declared unlawful unless (killing it) is just (according to the law and decree of the court). But whoever is killed unjustly, We have indeed given their heir the right of retribution according to the legal procedure), but they too must not exceed the limits in (retributive) killing. He/she is indeed helped (by God, the responsibility of his/ her legal help and support will be on the government).[159]

It is from this verse that the principle of proportionality in Islamic international humanitarian law is derived. Even when killing is justified, this principle would assert the importance of staying within the corpus of justice and mercy that is firmly rooted in the principles of the faith. Therefore, we see the ideas of justice and mercy doing the moral work in justifying and delineating the contours of the proportionality principle—as understood in Islamic law.

The conduct and use of ammunition in an unethical manner has also been proscribed in the Islamic tradition. There is a narration according to Abu Hurayra (a famous companion of the Prophet Muhammad), which states:

> Abu-al-Qasim said: "Whoever points a piece of iron at his brother, the angels will curse him until he puts it down, even if he [the one at whom it is pointed] is his brother of the same father and mother." [160]

In another narration, the Prophet Muhammad has affirmed this—stating that nobody should point a weapon at his brother.[161] From these examples, we see that there is a typification of the ethics and conduct that need to be observed in terms of the use of weaponry in a non-combatant situation, as well as when engaged in a legitimate war.

The killing of non-Muslim citizens, without commission of a crime, is also categorically prohibited. According to Abd Allah b. Amar, the Prophet Muhammad said:

> Anyone who kills a non-Muslim citizen will not smell the fragrance of Paradise, even though its fragrance can be smelt at a distance of forty years.[162]

The same point is emphasised by Abu Bakra, Prophet Muhammad said:

> Anyone who unjustly kills a non-Muslim under a treaty (*mu'ahad*) will be forbidden to smell the fragrance of Paradise, even though its fragrance can be smelt at a distance of a hundred years.[163]

Islamic international humanitarian law prohibits the unlawful killing of someone who accepts Islam in the midst of fighting.[164] In another narration, the Prophet Muhammad forbade the killing of a person of no faith if he should say that "There is no god but God."[165] In another narration where a person of no faith[166] engaged in the battlefield took refuge behind a tree and said, "I have surrendered to God", the Prophet Muhammad said: "No. Do not kill him. If you were to kill him, then he would be in your position [i.e., Muslim] before you killed him and you would be in his position [i.e., a person of no faith] before he said that word which he said."[167]

The brutal way in which terrorists engage in killing, as well as in the pillaging and destruction of sacred places of worship, educational institutions, hospitals, markets, and public spaces, is categorically at odds with the merciful and benevolent teaching expounded by Prophet Muhammad. The example mentioned above amply demonstrates that the life of an enemy on the battlefield is protected when they accept faith.

Those who act as accomplices by providing material and financial support to acts of terrorism are also called out by the Prophet Muhammad in a narration reported by Abu Hurayra:

> If anyone helps in the murder of a believer-even if with only a few words— he/she will meet God with the words written on his forehead: "hopeless of God's mercy."[168]

There is a categorical condemnation of those who subject Muslims to burning through explosions and other means. Their resting place will be in hell in The Qur'an:

> Indeed, those who subject the believing men and women to tribulation [*fatanu*] and then do not repent, for them is the punishment of Hell, and for them is a burning torment.[169]

The great scholars of Qur'anic exegesis, such as Imam Fakhr al-Din al-Razi, interpret the word *fatanu* as "burning in fire."[170] This is expounded on further by the great Imam, stating:

> Both punishments will occur in the Hereafter; however, the torment of the Hellfire will be on account of their disbelief, and the burning torment will be an additional punishment meted out to them on account of their burning of the believers.[171]

Islamic humanitarian law prohibits suicide outside of battle, as well as during a battle. The Qur'an stipulates: "And do not cast yourselves into destruction with your own hands and adopt righteousness. Verily, God loves the righteous."[172] The verse is further endorsed by the passage: "and do not kill yourselves."[173] Al-Razi expounds on this by stating that it "proves that it is unlawful for one to kill someone else or oneself unjustly."[174]

There are numerous hadiths that also categorically prohibit the act of suicide. The Prophet Muhammad explicitly declared the act of suicide forbidden when he said, "The one who commits suicide will go to hell and will keep falling into it and will abide there forever."[175]

In another narration Thabit b. al-Dahhak reported that the Prophet Muhammad said that "Whoever kills himself with something will be tormented by it in the Hellfire."[176]

Islamic humanitarian law categorically condemns the leaders who command others to commit suicide. The Prophet Muhammad stated that "There is no obedience in that which is disobedience. Obedience is only in that which is right."[177] Islamic humanitarian law also categorically prohibits those who commit suicide on the battlefield, by sharing a powerful reflective instruction:

Indeed, a man will do the acts of the people of Paradise—insomuch as it appears to people—even though he is from the denizens of the Fire; and indeed, a man will do the acts of the people of the Fire—insomuch as it appears to people—even though he is from the people of Paradise.[178]

The indiscriminate killing of innocent people is categorically prohibited in Islamic humanitarian law. Killing Muslims or non-Muslims as a principle of equality and humanity is also prohibited.[179] The protection of life, property and honour is sacrosanct, and is affirmed in the last Sermon of the Prophet Muhammad:

> Indeed your blood and your property and your honour are inviolable, like the inviolability of this day of yours and this month of yours and this land of yours until the day you meet your Lord.[180]

The principles of justice and mercy resonate continuously as part of Islamic humanitarian law.

There is thus a very high barometer set in Islamic humanitarian law, condemning acts of terrorism, the indiscriminate killing of innocents, and even acts of violence against those who are not of the Islamic faith during wartime.

At the heart of Islamic humanitarian law is the principle of "justice", as mentioned in the Qur'anic dictum:

> O you who believe! Stand firm from God, witness in justice, and do not let the hatred of a people prevent you from being just. Be just; that is closer to righteousness. And fear God. Indeed, God is Well-Informed of what you do.[181]

The verse instils the principle of equanimity in Islamic humanitarian law and urges individuals to observe balance in dealing with nation states by avoiding acts of repression or the transgression of the limits and boundaries of moral and humane acceptability. Justice here is equated closely with the concept of righteousness. Justice thus entails goodness and right conduct for action. This indicates that acting justly, under the Islamic tradition, is a core moral value.

The condemnation of the indiscriminate killing of innocents is set out in the following verse:

> God does not forbid you of those who do not fight you because of religion and do not expel you from your homes- from being righteous towards them and treating them justly. Indeed, God loves the just.[182]

The passage reaffirms the universal concept of justice that is enshrined in Islamic ethics, rules, and engagement of war. Furthermore, as part of the umbrella of Islamic humanitarian law, the killing of children is prohibited,[183] as is that of women and old men.

In a prophetic narration (reported by Ahmad h. Hanbal in *Al-Musnad*) it is mentioned:

> Break no promise, steal not from the spoils of war and do not mutilate the bodies or slay children or monks.

Sanctity, Safety and Protection of Missing Persons

The sanctity of the natural environment, along with the safety and protection of non-combatants, has been addressed in the Islamic tradition by the companions and pious scholars of early Islamic history. The protection of the natural environment and habitat is of critical importance in a combat situation. In one narration, Yahya b. Sa'id states that he was told that while bidding farewell to the Muslim forces bound for Syria, Abu Bakr al-Siddiq came to Yazid b. Abi Sufyan and told him:

> I command you to observe ten things: Do not kill a young child, a woman or an elderly infirm man. Do not cut down fruit-bearing trees or demolish buildings. Do not slaughter a sheep or a camel except for food. Do not drown or burn date-palm trees. And do not steal from the war booty or show cowardice. [185]

In another narration, according to Said b. al Musayyib, Abu Bakr al-Siddiq said while sending troops to Syria under the leadership of Yazid b. Abi Sufyan, Amr b. Al-As and Shurahbil b. Hasna:

> Neither sow corruption in the land nor defy what you are commanded to do. Do not drown or burn date palm trees. Do not kill any animal. Do not cut down a fruit bearing tree. Do not demolish a church. And do not kill any children or old people or women. Soon you shall come upon people who have secluded themselves in cloisters; you must leave them to engage in that for they have secluded themselves. (Malik, Abd al-Razzaq and al-Bayhaqi).[186]

To further endorse the above narration, al-Hindi reiterates that the men should "not kill a sick person or a priest."[187]

The ethics of observance set out in Islamic humanitarian law set the highest moral compass and framework to be observed. An important point mentioned by classical Islamic scholars in terms of the rules and engagement of battle, is that individuals should adhere to treaty obligations and pacts and avoid breaching such obligations. An example of this is that of the *dhimmi* contract. Imam al-Qarafi al-Maliki explains that the *dhimmi* contract concluded with the *dhimmis* (non-Muslims) established certain rights that non-Muslims had towards Muslims. Hence, Muslims ensure that they keep the non-Muslim citizens protected in their proximity under the bountiful obligation of their rights prescribed by their Lord, the Prophet Muhammad, and the religion of Islam. There is an obligation for the "Islamic State" to protect *dhimmis* if they are attacked—for instance, if the aggressors intrude on the boundaries of the "Islamic State", it is incumbent on the "Islamic State" to fight the aggressors. Handing them over to the aggressors without defending their rights and obligations will be deemed as sheer negligence and a breach of the *dhimmi* contract obligations.[188]

International Islamic humanitarian law prohibits the killing of non-combatants during a war. This includes groups such as farmers,[189] women and children.[190] The only groups that are allowed to be killed are those that are partaking in active combat.[191] Abd al-Razzaq Juwaybir reported that a woman from the tribe of Banu Asad informed him that she heard Ammar declare after the Caliph Ali had finished the Battle of the Camel (656 CE):

> Do not kill an injured person and do not enter the house of someone who has laid down his arms, for he is considered safe. Similarly, the one who shuts his door is considered safe.[192]

The tenets of Islamic international humanitarian law can also be observed in the military ethics and the code of conduct observed during battle. It is forbidden, for instance, to wage night offensives against the enemy. Imam al-Bukhari and Imam Muslim narrated on the authority of Anas b. Malik who said:

> The Prophet Muhammad came to Khaybar at night, and when he came to a people [a force] at night, he would not attack them until daybreak.[193]

It is prohibited to burn another individual in Islamic humanitarian law as the Prophet Muhammad declared that "It is not fitting that anyone but the Lord of the fire should punish with the fire."[194] It is also prohibited to enter to enter the home of an enemy and loot them as the Prophet Muhammad said, "God has not permitted you to enter the houses of the People of the Book without permission, or to beat their women, or to eat their fruit".[195]

As part of the ethical norms of warfare under Islamic humanitarian law, the Prophet Muhammad stated, "There is no jihad for the one who breaks into the houses of others or loots people on the road."[196] It is prohibited to destroy cattle, crops, and the properties of opponents under Islamic international humanitarian law. Imam al-Tirmidhi quoted the following saying from the first Caliph:

> Abu Bakr al-Siddiq forbade people from cutting down fruit bearing trees or destroying buildings [during war] and the Muslims abided by his instructions after that.[197]

To conclude this section on the importance that international Islamic humanitarian law places on preserving the natural habitat, Abd Allah b. Umar states in one narration that when Abu Bakr al-Siddiq dispatched the Muslim troops to Syria, he walked with them for two miles and addressed them, saying:

> I enjoin you to fear God. Do not disobey the (military commander) or show cowardice. Do not drown date-palm trees or set crops on fire. Do not hobble animals and do not cut down fruit bearing trees. Do not kill an old man or a young child.[198]

The idea here is that those elements of our lives that our immensely *vulnerable* to us—the environment, animals, old persons, young children—should not be hurt or treated as collaterals in combat situations. At the heart of the rules of warfare resides the fundamental tenet of protecting innocents, the natural habitat, and the environment. The sanctity, safety, and dignity of human beings not engaged in battle is deemed sacrosanct to the extent that these individuals must be treated humanely.[199]

Diplomacy Within the Islamic Tradition

International Islamic humanitarian law also applies to the rules and engagements of international states, diplomatic accords, protection, understanding and norms. Safeguarding the lives of diplomats, foreign emissaries, and representatives is part of the core teaching of the Prophet Muhammad. Abd Allah b. Masud stated: "It is an established Sunna that ambassadors are not to be killed."[200]

A key component of international diplomacy in international Islamic humanitarian law is the way in which war is openly declared against another state. This has been more commonly understood via the word "Jihad." It is important to stress that in international Islamic humanitarian law, *Jihad* can be declared only by a state, and not by a non-state actor. The concept of *Jihad* is an oft-misunderstood term by those who are not well versed in the modalities of Islamic law. Lexically, its meaning emanated from the word "*juhd*", which means to strive and exert effort to pursue a noble endeavour. In the corpus of Islamic spirituality, it also includes striving against one's base desires, to which the Prophet Muhammad gave a higher station than that of physical exertion on the battlefield.

Owing to a lack of reliance on state practice in the earthly formulation of the legal framework, scholars played a major role in translating Islamic sources into a legal system. Contemporary scholarship, however, has not given sufficient emphasis to the roles played by the scholars. Many focused on the similarities or differences between Islamic law and international humanitarian law. In so doing, they ignored the processes of scholarly development of the law and focused on the outcomes.[201]

Unlike international law, Islamic law does not address the matter of the conduct of hostilities as a distinct area of law, as with international humanitarian law. This complicates the task of the scholar of Islamic law. There is a need for knowledge about Islamic law and the protection of civilians and the Islamic legal heritage in order to comprehend fully the rules governing armed conflict.[202]

Islamic laws of war are divided into four main subcategories: fighting non-Muslims who are not followers of one of the holy religions; fighting scriptuaries (believers in one of the holy books including the Torah, and the Bible, and, according to some, the Zoroastrians); fighting apostates; and fighting Muslims in revolt. Islamic laws of war are also governed by divine law; binding Muslims in their dealing, conduct, and relationships with others.[203]

Since international humanitarian law (IHL) is a part of international law, and is accordingly organised around the notion of sovereignty, state interest is of great importance. As stated by the International Red Cross, IHL was formulated when "[s]tates have agreed to a series of practical rules, based on the bitter experience of modern warfare. These rules strike a careful balance between humanitarian concerns and the military requirements of States." This pragmatic system, collectively agreed by the sovereign states who were parties to IHL's legal instruments, has served these states' interests and regulated war to the extent that was possible. On the other hand, Islamic jurisprudence is representative of a divine law, "aspiring to establish on earth the kingdom of God." As an area of a divine law, rather than promoting the shared objectives of sovereign states, Islamic laws of war possess a universal inclusive agenda and thus aim for the promotion of the Islamic mission, with supreme importance laid on the interest of Muslims.[204]

This discrepancy in the treatment of armed conflict can be attributed to the foundational difference between the two regimes, mentioned earlier. In the case of IHL, states were interested in regulating warfare among themselves, but were reluctant to dismiss their sovereignty to the degree of allowing internal groups to threaten or destabilise them at the domestic level. Islamic law, however, originating from the divine and articulated by jurists, was more willing to grant legitimacy to rebellion because of Islamic law's important mission of protecting Muslim subjects. The life and property of a Muslim—even if that Muslim was a rebel—are sacred and cannot be threatened.

Sarakhsī, a Hanafi scholar and the compiler of Shaybani's Siyar, stated that apostate women should not be killed. Furthermore, Sarakhsī set a qualification for killing apostates, which is being given a chance to repent and refusing to do so. Contrary to Shāfi'ī's silence on legitimacy of rebellion, Sarakhsī adopted a more reserved position on rebellion. His section on rebellion is titled "Khawārij". The Khawārij started with a group of fighters who rejected Ali's acceptance of arbitration in the first *fitna* and are generally perceived to have committed a major sin for doing so.[205]

Mālikis, Hanafīs, and Shāfi'ī held that women and children may not be targeted in war, because the Prophet Muhammad gave instructions not to kill women and children. Scholars have interpreted this particular prohibition to be a prohibition on targeting, rather than on killing.

Rebellion

The discourse on the Islamic law on rebellion become more pertinent during the Arab Uprisings, which commenced in 2011.

El Fadl argues that the law of rebellion, as a systematic and coherent body of discourse, in all probability developed in the late second/eighth century and continued to be restated, rearticulated, and reconstructed within the same framework until the eleventh/seventeenth century.[206] It is also noteworthy that the juristic discourses on rebellion have received very little attention in both non-Muslim and Muslim modern scholarship.

One of the basic and most essential functions of law is to resolve conflicts and maintain order. The perpetuation of order is a core function of law. Law aspires to resolve conflict and uphold stability and order. It is also a method of social engineering to achieve social results. El Fadl argues that the values of order, stability, and conflict resolution are strongly ingrained in a legal culture.[207] A legal system does not easily endorse a state of anarchy or the potential for instability.

The second and third duties are concerned with preserving order and resolving conflict. The second duty is to implement the law as to litigants, and to resolve conflicts so that justice may prevail. The third duty is to keep the peace and guarantee security so that people may safely go about their affairs.[208]

There are Muslim jurists who have argued that an unjust ruler is illegitimate. In fact, they stress that an unjust ruler is the real rebel, and not those who refuse to yield to injustice.

The word "Baghat" is used in a non-technical fashion to signify that all Muslims will cooperate against any unjust or offending party. Nevertheless, despite its apparent significance, this precedent is hardly ever cited in Islamic legal sources. Rather, it is the Qur'anic verse on the subject that is cited in nearly every discourse on rebellion, and which states:

> If two parties among the believers fight each other, then make peace between them. But if one of them transgresses (baghat) against the other, then fight, all of you, against the one that transgresses until it complies with the command of God. But if it complies, then make peace between the two parties with justice and be fair, for God loves those who are fair and just. The believers are but a single brotherhood. So, reconcile your two [contending] brothers, and fear God so that you will receive His mercy. [209]

Conflicts Between Two Equal Parties

The duty of a Muslim during a fitna (discord and strife), according to tradition, is to abstain from participating and to avoid supporting civil turmoil or strife. It is important to note, however, that this was not a discourse of political pacifism alone; after all, Caliph Ali, Aisha, and their supporters did take part in excursions, and their credibility also had to be upheld. For the most part, the fitna discourse served to restore what El Fadl termed the "psychic balance" of the Muslim nation by providing a means of explaining, justifying, and reconciling the conflicting positions of the Companions of the Prophet Muhammad in the early civil wars.[210]

It is stipulated in the Qur'an that:

> Those who wage war against God and His Prophet, and strive to cause corruption on earth, are to be punished by being exiled, killed, or crucified, or mutilated by having a hand and foot amputated. That is their disgrace in this world, and they will receive a heavy punishment in the Hereafter, except for those who repent before they can be captured.[211]

In the same passage, the importance of forgiveness for those that repent is fundamental to showing the doors of mercy are always open for those that mend their ways.

El Fadl argues that in the modern state, law is deterministic and positivistic in that obedience to the law is not premised on proof and persuasion, but on sovereign command and compulsion. Modern legal systems are thus fundamentally inconsistent with the epistemological foundations of the classical Islamic legal system.[212] The very idea of "Islamic law" is thus, in many ways, a misnomer. Although classical jurists (*fuqahā'*) adjudicated everything from prayers and fasting to war and trade, it is uncertain whether they were engaged in law-making as we understand law today. It would be more accurate to say that they were engaged in identifying norms derived from teachings inspired by the revelation, as well as the experiences of the early Muslim communities, and in describing how these practices translated into the realities of their own societies.

Moosa, on the other hand, suggests that we ought to think of "Islamic law as an enterprise in ethics."[213] El Fadl points out that, in his view, Islamic law is best described as the process of a practiced discipline of deliberative and purposeful practical reasoning in which rulings are developed primarily through analogical dynamics. Jurists have further insisted that Shari'a law is anchored on the twin pillars of the Qur'an and the Sunnah. It is important, however, to distinguish between the formal sources of law in the Islamic legal tradition and practical sources of law. Formal sources of law are an ideological construct—they are the ultimate foundations invoked by jurists and judges, as the basis of legal legitimacy and authority. The practical sources, however, are the actual premises and processes utilised in legal practice in the process of producing positive rules and commandments.

In theory, the foundations of all law in Islamic jurisprudence are the following: the Qur'an, the Sunnah (the tradition of the Prophet Muhammad and his companions), qiyas (analogical reasoning), and ijma (consensus or the overall agreement of Muslim jurists). In contrast to mainstream Sunni Islam, Shi'i jurisprudence, as well as a minority of Sunni jurists in the classical orientations, recognise reason (instead of qiyas) as a foundational source of law. These four are legitimating sources, but the practical sources of law include an array of conceptual tools that greatly expand the venues of the legal determination.[214]

Moreover, there is a classical tradition of disputations and debates on what is known as the "occasions of revelation" (*asbāb al-nuzūl*). These address the context that surrounded the revelation of Qur'anic verses or chapters, and the critical issue of abrogation (naskh), as well as which Qur'anic prescriptions and commandments, if any, were nullified or voided during the time of the Prophet Muhammad.

Shi'i jurists heavily relied on the teachings of the infallible imams, all of whom were the descendants of Ali, the fourth Caliph and cousin of Prophet Muhammad, and his wife Fatima, the Prophet's daughter. It is important to note that respect and reverence for the descendants of the Prophet Muhammad is also a core tenet of Sunni creed and methodology. It is fair to say that the Qur'an and the Sunnah are the two primary, formal sources of legitimacy in Islamic law. There is also the canopy of usul (principles of jurisprudence) from which the Islamic legal scholars developed their methodologies and schools of jurisprudence to derive rulings.

Pluralism is, thus, one of the foundational ideas of Islamic jurisprudence, variously attributed to the eponyms of the Hanafi and Shafi'i schools of law. Abu Hanifa (d. 150/767) and al-Shafi'i asserted:

> We believe that our opinions are correct, but we are always cognizant of the fact that our opinions may be wrong. We also believe that the opinions of our opponents are wrong, but we are always cognizant of the fact that they may be correct.[215]

For instance, it is firmly established in the Islamic legal tradition that Shari'a seeks to protect and promote five fundamental values: 1) life; 2) intellect; 3) reputation or dignity; 4) lineage or family; and 5) property. These are among the five objectives constituting Maqāṣid al-Shari'a, or part of the five core purposes of Shari'a. The core of Islamic law thus rests on adherence to these principles.

Through the course of this chapter, it has been established that the sources and principles of conflict resolution, arbitration and peacekeeping based on Islamic International Law have at their core the protection, preservation, and promotion of humanity based on principles of justice, human rights, reconciliation, and mercy. If we engage closely with the ideas developed here, we see that international law, at a global scale, can be informed by these valuable perspectives from Islamic law and thought—rooted in the most core human values.

References

Ali, S.S. *Modern Challenges to Islamic Law*. Cambridge: Cambridge University Press, 2019.

Cowan J.M., ed. *The Hans Wehr Dictionary of Modern Written Arabic*. New York: BN Publishing, 1999.

El Fadl, K. A. *Reasoning With God. Reclaiming Shari'ah in the Modern Age*. Washington, DC: Rowman and Littlefield, 2014.

El Fadl, K. A. *Rebellion and Violence in Islamic Law*. Cambridge: Cambridge University Press, 2001.

The Glorious Qur'an, translated by Shaykh-ul Islam Dr Muhammad Tahir-ul-Qadri. Minhaj al-Quran, 2012.

Badawi, N. "Islamic Jurisprudence and the Regulation of Armed Conflict." Program on Humanitarian Policy and Conflict Research, Harvard University, February 2009,

CHAPTER THREE

A COMPARATIVE ANALYSIS OF PEACE,
RECONCILIATION, CONFLICT RESOLUTION
AND ARBITRATION BASED ON SOURCES
OF PUBLIC INTERNATIONAL LAW
AND ISLAMIC LAW

Abstract

This chapter will undertake a comparative analysis of how the sources of Public International Law and Islamic Law demonstrate areas of convergence and divergence on the theme of Peace, Reconciliation, Conflict Resolution and Arbitration. It will also touch on the principles of Self-Defence, Acts of War-Aggression, Counter Terrorism and Security, the use of Arbitration tools, Treating of Prisoners of War, Hostages, Dialogue and Diplomatic tools, Use of Armaments along with the principle of Human Rights and Humanitarianism according to Public International and Islamic Law. The major goal of this chapter is to investigate the relationship between Public International Law and Islamic Law and to bring these two approaches into dialogue.

Islamic Law and International Law

The former vice president of the ICJ, Awn Shawkat Al-Khasawneh stated that "Islamic traditions and law are neither 'foreign' to international law nor are they different from 'Western' conceptions of law.[216] This statement demonstrates that there is an interface between the two pioneering modes of international jurisprudence and adjudication, that may not be readily apparent at first glance. On closer investigation, however, we find that the intersections of these two modes is extremely valuable for our understandings of peacebuilding and conflict resolution between nation-states.

The Sources of international law are exhaustively enumerated in Article 38 (1) of the Statute of the ICJ.[217] They include international conventions, treaties, international custom, general principles of law recognised by civilised nations, judicial decisions, and the teachings of the most highly qualified publicists.[218] Many of these sources of international law that focus on customary norms are *per se* secular in nature, even if indirectly or historically informed by Christian principles. Reliance on secular, religion-neutral arguments is an organising principle for all international decision-makers.[219]

The Islamic tradition, on the other hand, has its own distinctive way of thinking about international law. Powell poses the question of how *siyar*, Islamic international law, has contributed to the law of nations?[220] Has there been any flow of legal knowledge from the Islamic milieu to the West? While one cannot dispute Europe's contributions to classical international law, it is essential to be familiar with those influences stemming from Islam. In this area, as Awn Shawkat Al-Khasawneh notes, "the contribution of Islamic law was significant and revolutionary for its time. It prohibited the killing of non-combatants, enjoined respect for houses of worship, prohibited the cutting down of trees, [and] required proportionality in response to wrongs committed."[221] Powell alludes to this, noting that "the Islamic milieu has contributed many scholarly treatises on international law. In the Middle Ages, specifically at the end of the eighth century, Muhammad ibn al-Hasan al-Shaybani, a prominent Islamic jurist, penned an Introduction to the Law of Nations, long before the time of Grotius's *De Jure Belli ac Pacis* in 1625."[222]

With the transcendental shift in the migration of Muslims to many countries in the West, this dichotomy of "The Land of Islam" and the "Land of War" has gradually diminished in mainstream discourse. For instance, al-Zuhili writes that "this division has no textual support, for no provision is made for it either in the Qur'an or in the Hadith. It is instead a transient description of what happens when war flares up between Muslims and others."[223]

The Islamic system continues to push back against the Western law of nations and challenges the decisions of international courts. Modern international law, however, can derive some measure of authority from the Islamic realm, even when there are strong Islamic counter norms that leave little space or role for any secular legal system. Powell refers to Badr's thought, which is one I endorse, namely:

"Islam can make valuable contributions to the progressive development of the law in this universal international order. Certain basic principles of

Islamic international law lend themselves to consolidating and expanding the scope of international law." [224]

Whereas a sizeable portion of international law emerged as a product of pre-existing state practice, Shari'a imposes a distinct set of standards—standards which are, in their core, in God's Will. Islamic law has two primary written sources, the Qur'an and the Sunnah, and two analogous non-textual sources, ijma (consensus) and qiyas (analogical reasoning). The last two constitute analytical, methodological tools for determining the law and can be used as a supplement in cases where the primary sources are silent. The Qur'an is, according to the Muslim faith, the book of divine revelation of God's Will or Dictum, and as such is believed to be perfect in both composition and content and incorruptible.[225]

There is clear evidence that certain tenets of Islamic Law diverge from international law. However, some have advanced the argument that Islam is simply incompatible with the law of nations, projecting a continuing divergence between the two systems. This narrative tells a traditional story of irreconcilable opposites and advocates that effective dialogue between international and Islamic law constitutes, for the most part, a futile endeavour. Either Islamic law should be domesticated to international law, or vice versa.[226] What is clear from the brief coverage in this chapter thus far is that that Islamic law and international law are not fundamentally incompatible. On the contrary, there are many dimensions of convergence between them—some of which reach deep into the heart of peaceful conflict management and peacekeeping.

Difference

The Law of Nations, or International Law, may be defined as the body of rules and principles of action which are binding upon civilised states in their relations with one another."[227] If there is a common theme running between the two realms, it is, according to Powell, the predominantly secular character of classical international law and the predominantly religious nature of Islamic law.[228]

From a historical perspective, the contexts in which Christianity and Islam materialised were fundamentally different. Christianity was birthed in a world where a robust system of rules, Roman law, already existed. As the Christian church grew, the canon lawyers drew largely from Roman law—at this point a comprehensive and mature legal system—overlaying upon it the fundamentals of the Christian faith. According to Powell, Islam, on the other hand, had no a priori legal system to work with other than unwritten tribal customs.[229] Thus, legal and religious precepts developed in an intertwined and simultaneous way.[230] There is a caveat to the points made here, in the sense that with reference to the evolutionary cycle of the Abrahamic faith traditions, Islam is seen as the final major revelatory world religion in this series and, hence, logically there are commonalities in the legal exegesis and structures with Christianity and Judaism.[231]

Several key figures of the Roman Church contributed immensely to the theory of the law of nations. For instance, while developing his thoughts on the causes and conduct of war, Augustine drew largely from the Roman legal tradition while imbuing it with Christian teachings.[232] Francisco de Vitoria, a sixteenth-century canon lawyer, Dominican priest, and theologian, was another key scholar of international law.[233]

According to Rosenne,

> In the medieval period proper, largely under the influence of Saint Augustine and others of the Church Fathers, the undifferentiated concepts of international law and international morality were conceived as part of the discipline of theology, and in that form international law germinated within the framework of the feudal system.[234]

We thus see that international law, as it emerged and developed in the West, has deep roots in the Christian faith.

There have been changes in the law over time, as opposed to immutable and divine truths as the basis for law. Grotius, whose comprehensive work *On the Law of War and Peace* (1625) encouraged the establishment of the interstate legal order, promoted fundamental principles of the Christian teaching.[235] Although his work contains references to diverse cultures and philosophies, Grotius's optimistic view of people's ability to do good was grounded in the spirit of Christianity. [236]After Grotius, international law continued to evolve in a dynamic way, moving steadily away from religious texts and doctrines. In their place, reason, logic, and secular rational calculations and philosophies became the benchmark for the establishment and interpretation of international law. Scholarly writers such as Christian Wolff (1679–1754) and Emmerich de Vattel (1714–1767) elaborated numerous aspects of international law. The hope of preventing future wars fought on religious grounds was a major motivation for Vattel. Interestingly, he accepted that international treaties can be concluded between peoples of different faiths:

> Different people treat with each other in the quality of men, and not under the character of Christians and Mahommedans. Their common safety requires that they should be capable of treating with each other and treating with security.[237]

The rise of the principle of state sovereignty reflected the desire of states to stipulate their legal requirements in a more clear and precise way, by means of written agreements. To a large degree, as Armstrong and colleagues argue:[238]

> the reality of Westphalia was that a decisive shift had been made toward the positivist principle that international law was what a society of sovereign states consented. Simply put, Westphalia was significant for its "secularisation of legitimacy.[239]

Therefore, we see that international law has evolved from its religious origins to become a largely secular legal system.

In contrast, the connection between religion and law is hardly subtle in traditional Shari'a: law, which is centred on religion—drawing exclusively from religious texts and doctrines. While these differences exist, it is also true that quite often, scholarly discourse and the world of policy have created an artificial demarcation between these two legal systems. Quite the opposite is in fact true: these two inherently dynamic and ever-evolving legal systems also share greater similarities than have commonly been assumed.

Custom

It is challenging to establish whether the psychological component of a customary rule indeed exists. This continues to be a complex determination in the realm of international law. Statesmen and diplomats often do not explicitly declare that their actions are in line with international law, or, indeed, that they believe a certain expectation or pattern of behaviour to be in alignment with the law.[240]

In its jurisprudence, the ICJ[241] has confirmed that custom is by no means obsolete as a source of states' legal obligations. In fact, some scholars argue that custom is enjoying a revival in international law. While it used to be considered an emblem of international law's conservatism and lack of progress, custom has since become a vehicle for evolutionary change demonstrating the adaptability of treaty rules and obligations to the divergent needs of the community of states in today's polity.[242]

Islamic scholars are the foundation stone of Shari'a. They discover what the law is, and mould Shari'a into well-defined rules and principles. As Hallaq writes, schools of jurisprudence—madhabs—in essence "produced law and afforded its axis of authority."[243] In the Islamic legal tradition, urf—custom or usage—although strictly speaking not a source of law, constitutes an important cradle of legal obligations. Islamic law stipulates that anything that respects the limits established by God is permitted. Customary norms of behaviour often fill in this legal lacuna. The literal meaning of urf is "something that is known", that is, the practices of Muslims.

Rule of Law Convergence

Conceptually, the term "rule of law" denotes a set of norms and principles strongly associated with legality and broader notions of justice. It is a vehicle for establishing and systematising authority. According to Dicey, rule of law comprises three basic elements: the unquestionable supremacy of law as opposed to the use of arbitrary power, equality in the eyes of the law for all citizens and government, and the primacy of the judicial process.[244]

The core definition of the rule of law, across cultural and political context, is that law must apply to everybody in an equal way, including to the sovereign. Even the sovereign is held accountable by the rule of law under this system, and this prevents state powers from being exercised in an arbitrary manner. Apart from this, the rule of law also requires that laws must be clear and accessible.[245]

Under Shari'a, judges were required to follow the law in their decisions and no ruler could interfere in this judicial process. In a way, judicial independence was the cornerstone of Islamic Law. Judicial decisions were held in the utmost esteem, regardless of the ranking of the judge. At the same time, because it was the jurists who were expounding upon law, the state itself was "a state under the law". The judicial mechanism also acted as a way to put checks and balances upon the sovereign and ensure that the sovereign was also held accountable under the rule-based legal system. This speaks to the overarching idea under this system that scholars, the state, and the people were to operate within legal limits established by God. We see this principle stated in the Qur'an which states "Be faithful to your pledge to God, when you enter into a pact."[246] The final authority—to which all stakeholders in any social or legal system were answerable to—was the authority of God.

Divergence from Peace

Oaths remain an essential part of religious adjudication in several international legal systems, especially in cases where testimonies or notarised documents of the litigating parties are contradictory. Disputants may also use a holy oath if there is a lack of evidence supporting their claims. In court, oaths have no established form and it is up to the judge to require that either one or both parties take the vow. To highlight their gravity, holy oaths used in litigation are commonly taken in the presence of two notaries at a local shrine, or a mosque. Thus, "it is not unusual for an individual to maintain a particular testimony right up to the moment of oath-taking and then to stop, refuse the oath, and surrender the case."[247]

Article 53 of the *Vienna Convention*[248] provides a definition of jus cogens as a norm which is "accepted and recognised by the international community of states as a norm from which no derogation is permitted and which can be modified only by a subsequent norm of general international law having the same character."[249]

Dawoody expounds on this point, as described by Ibn Qayyim al-Jawziyyah (d. 1350). Serving the public interest is the objective of every single rule in Islam, because Shari'a is founded on the divine command and the public good of the people in this world and the next.

"The term siyar is also used by some Ḥanafī jurists to refer to the rules governing certain types of non-international armed conflict (NIAC) that occurred in the first half of the first Islamic century. These include what are known in Islamic jurisprudence as *qitāl al-bughāh* (fighting against rebels or secessionists) and *ḥurūb al-riddah* (wars of apostasy)." [250]

L.C. Green, in his book *The Contemporary Law of Armed Conflict*,[251] demonstrates that Jewish and ancient Chinese, Indian, and Greek civilisations developed numerous restraints on warfare. Jurists gave conflicting rulings regarding the permissibility of, for example, targeting women, children, or the elderly if they engaged in hostilities, along with the use of certain methods of warfare.[252] The Old Testament states that it is prohibited to destroy trees[253] or kill captives, and that food and water should be provided to captives until they are set free. In ancient Chinese civilisation, the general and military strategist Sun Tzu (d. 496 BCE)[254] stressed that only enemy armies are to be attacked, and that cities are to be attacked only where there is no alternative. In ancient India, the list of prohibitions during armed conflict includes attacking a sleeping enemy, desecration of corpses, killing those who are physically or mentally incapacitated and, like the Greek civilisation, the use of poisoned weapons. Islamic law also drew a distinction between international and non-international conflicts, even though it did not use the same terms.

NIACs are divided into four categories according to the Muslim jurists: *ḥurūb alriddah* (wars of apostasy); *qitāl al-bughāh* (fighting against rebels or secessionists); *ḥirābah* (fighting against bandits, highway robbers, terrorists, or pirates); and *qitāl al-khawārij* (fighting against violent religious fanatics). In Islamic law, the distinction between these types of war is important because the rules of war differ from one category to another.[255]

When talking about the purpose of her own book on this subject, Powell affirms that:

> "Notwithstanding its contributions to this literature, this study intended to add insights principally to the scholarship on international law, in particular the emerging study of comparative international law. Indeed, understanding how different countries and—more broadly—different domestic legal traditions interpret and conceive of international law is a scholarly effort worth pursuing." [256]

This is an endeavour and statement I very much endorse and concur with. Building on Powell's analysis, my aim is to specifically highlight how understanding tenets of Islamic law helps contextualise international law and its developments in a unique manner—which can ultimately inform both policy and practice.

International Islamic Law: Perceptions and Reality

It is also important to undertake a comparative exercise in search of legal areas where the Islamic legal tradition and international law coexist without conflict, and legal areas where these two systems diverge. A discussion of such legal traits inherently rests on the description of laws and customs.

Comparatively speaking, the Islamic legal tradition is more diverse than other legal traditions, because the balance between religious laws and secular laws is subject to frequent renegotiation. In Iran, there is the concept of religious guardianship *"Velayat e Faqih"*—of the Judiciary, legislature, and executive branches. The most recent constitution of the Maldives is explicit in its references to Islamic identity. Article 10 (a) declares that "the religion of the State of the Maldives is Islam. Islam shall be one of the basis of all the laws of the Maldives." Article 10 (b) states that "No law contrary to any tenet of Islam shall be enacted in the Maldives."[257] Therefore, we see that the constitution here is religious in spirit and sees Islamic identity as central to the legal imagination in the nation.

With the realm of international law, we see according to Powell that Hans Kelsen, a proponent of the Just War doctrine, revived many ideas earlier expressed by Augustine, Thomas Aquinas, and Grotius. He developed the concept of the Grundnorm, or ultimate norm that provides an underlying basis for a legal system.[258]

There is a strong synergy between international law and its underlying values. As Shaw writes:

A Comparative Analysis of Peace, Reconciliation, Conflict Resolution and Arbitration Based on Sources of Public International and Islamic Law

"Just as any domestic community must have a background of ideas and hopes to aim at, even if few can be or are ever attained, so the international community, too, must bear in mind its ultimate values." [259]

It is important to emphasise, however, that although the intertwining of morality and religion constituted an important basis for the building of the laws and the state's authority, the Muslim world has quickly introduced the institutional differentiation of state and religion. With this in mind, Weiss explains:

"Although the law is of divine provenance, the actual construction of the law is a human activity, and its results represent the law of God as humanly understood. Since the law does not descend from heaven ready-made, it is the human understanding of the law—the human fiqh—that must be normative for society."[260] It is this human agency that, according to An-Na'im, enables the Islamic law to "engage international law as an integral aspect of the context and experience of those societies." [261]

In this context, Bassiouni writes,

"The Qur'ān contains the expressions of values, principles, and guidelines for conduct, admonitions against prohibited and wrongful conduct, and exhortations to do good and abjure evil. In that sense, it is all-inclusive, but not as legal prescriptions and proscriptions." [262]

Sunnah, the second main source of law, comprises traditions, acts, and words of the Prophet Muhammad. The word "Sunnah" literally means a pattern of behaviour, a manner of acting, a rule of conduct. If the Qur'an does not speak on a given issue, the Sunnah is used to provide guidance.[263]

There are also substantive and procedural areas where Islamic law and international law differ, insofar as they lack analogous concepts. The preferences of the international legal system toward international conflict management mechanisms relay an interesting story about the dual pull of Islamic law and secular law within ILS' domestic legal systems. If one is to develop a meaningful understanding of how peaceful settlement works, one must gain knowledge of differences and similarities between the Islamic legal tradition and classical international law.[264] The former can greatly inform how conflict management is imagined and conducted in the latter. Bearing this in mind, we can now delve deeper into how peace and reconciliation are dealt with under both Islamic and International law—and examine the several nuances at play here.

Peace and Reconciliation in Islamic and International Law

The hadith of the Prophet Muhammad and other sources teach that Muslims are brothers and constitute a brotherhood.[265] Muslim countries, therefore, should not be hostile to each other. They should instead attempt to conciliate.

Powell elucidates on the relationship between the Islamic milieu and international law and its institutions by exclaiming that this relationship is context specific: "it hinges fundamentally on the domestic legal system of each of the ILS [International Legal System]."[266] Different international conflict management methods appeal to different components of the ILS, depending on each one's domestic legal system. Powell points out that the answer to the "Shari'a-international law nexus puzzle" lies in the diversity of how secular laws and religious laws fuse in domestic legal systems across the Islamic milieu. In other words, not all international legal systems are Islamic to the same degree or in the same way.[267]

There are many instances in which Islamic law points in one direction and Western-based, secularised international law points in another. Yet, this conflict is partially eased by the reality of Islamic law itself. There is material from within Islamic law to show that the cannon can be interpreted in a manner that bears similarities with central ideas in international law. As disconcerting as the dissonance between Islamic law and international law may seem, there are more similarities between these two legal systems than the policy world, as well as scholarly forums, account for.[268]

Intrinsically, one of the most elaborate constitutional references of this kind is that of the Afghan 1980 Constitution, which declared that "the Democratic Republic of Afghanistan will make efforts on the basis of good intentions and the principle of peaceful co-existence to help resolve justly and peacefully all the existing unsettled problems among neighbouring countries in the region."[269] Although this constitution draws from Islamic law and its tenets, it focuses on core principles such as the principle of peaceful co-existence that feature significantly in international law and peacekeeping practices.

The number of mentions of the words of *"Shari'a"-"Islam"* in the Constitution of Muslim majority countries, as laid out by Powell, is represented by the following:

- Between 0–10 mentions: Morocco, Comoros, Gambia, Algeria, Tunisia, Libya, Sudan, Iraq, Egypt, Syria, Lebanon, Kuwait, Qatar, United Arab Emirates, Oman, Indonesia, Bangladesh;

- Between 11–33 mentions: Mauritania, Jordan, Yemen, Bahrain, Brunei, Afghanistan;
- Between 34–209 mentions: Iran, Saudi Arabia, Nigeria, Malaysia, Maldives, Pakistan, Mauritania, Comoros, Algeria, Tunisia, Libya, Sudan.[270]

This shows how Shari'a law has influenced a great many domestic legal systems. There is also a view in international discourse pertaining to whether Islamic law matters in the widely adopted Western model with an assertion that government and state are de jure and de facto "religion-neutral."[271] How can this perceived neutrality be reconciled with the explicit religious undertones of some laws? These are open questions that require further investigation. But what we can conclude is that peace and reconciliation are discussed, often in similar ways, in Islamic law and international legal discourse.

Conflict Resolution and Arbitration in Islamic and International Law

Arbitration is a relatively popular method for resolving interstate conflicts, and it gained traction particularly in the period following the Jay Treaty of 1794 between Great Britain and the United States.[272] Within arbitration, oaths of a religious nature are not part of the lexical discourse of modern international law. Arbitration between city-states in ancient Greece, one of the earliest instances of interstate dispute settlement, quickly moved away from settlement by the Olympian gods, or a common religious body. The arbitration process traversed mostly to one based on secular logic.

In contrast, oaths of a deeply religious nature continue to hold a privileged position in Islamic law. They appealed to Arabs who, as the Qur'an's primary audience, were well acquainted with oaths as a method for making credible commitments. The Qur'an repeatedly speaks about the process of oath-taking. For instance, Chapter 16, verse 94 reads: "Take not your oaths as mere mutual deceit." This verse underlines the community-based and relational character of Shari'a—wherein individuals are seen as being constituted by the community and their relationships with other members, and therefore are held accountable through oaths. The Constitution of Medina was an oath-bound agreement.[273]

International, non-binding third-party procedures such as mediation and conciliation are similar to Shari'a-based dispute resolution in terms of procedure.[274] The Islamic legal tradition focuses on mediation and reconciliation. Secular laws are embedded in these international legal systems whereas domestic laws form a natural bridge with international courts and arbitration tribunals. These venues include the ICJ; its predecessor, the Permanent Court of International Justice (PCIJ); the World Trade Organization dispute settlement; and international mediation.

The relationship between the Islamic system and the Court—the main UN judicial organ—provides a test for the universality of a major mode of dispute settlement. International law, including its formalised institutions, continues to develop and adjust to the requirements of the contemporary international community. If international law is to be regarded as an effective tool for upholding global peace, the several structural biases embedded in peaceful resolution fora must be mitigated. Effectiveness in this domain entails going beyond the power of symbolic authority and legitimacy and fostering true agreement and compliance. Following from this, I agree with Powell on the following view:

> "International law and the Islamic legal tradition as dynamic and evolving legal traditions both have transformative potential that if realised can bring about a more peaceful world." [275]

Imam Ibrahim Amin has stressed that:

> "Looking at Islamic law via secular lenses does not work well. There is a risk of imposing the general perspective of secular law on Islamic law. He would rather call it the moral code, [the] Islamic moral code as such."[276]

It is thus important to retain the contextual and cultural specificity of Islamic law, even when applying it to other areas of law and practice.

International Islamic Law (siyar)

Al Ghunaimi adds that while "a large element in Muslim International law is increasingly conventional," it is also crucial to take into consideration "the usul, sources of the Shari'a, for primary evidence of the Muslim law of nations."[277]

Islamic law has, for centuries, coexisted alongside Western international law. The ongoing interaction between the two systems has revealed some important doctrinal differences, as well as points of convergence, that influence the preferences of ILS towards international conflict management strategies. For instance, although fitting in the category of Muslim states, Turkey—despite its overwhelmingly Muslim population—cannot be classified as part of the ILS because its official legal system is secular.[278] The Islamic Republic of Pakistan has been the official name of Pakistan since its 1956 constitution, but Shari'a's place in the Pakistani legal system is quite different from that of Saudi Arabia, whose 1992 Basic Law of Governance declares the Kingdom a fully sovereign Arab Islamic State.[279] In fact, according to the Malaysian constitution, the states and territories have the right to decide which interpretation of Islamic law to follow.[280]

Powell's theory draws a direct link between laws within states and laws regulating interactions between states. The balance of religious laws and secular laws defines each of the ILS domestic legal systems. Islamic scholarship diverges on whether the consensus must be shared by the entire community of Muslims or by the community of scholars, in part or in whole. But the most widely accepted view is that the presence of consensus is ascertained by "an absence of known objection to the expressed opinion of a single mujtahid."[281]

Counter Terrorism and Security Based on Sources of Public International Law and International Islamic Law

As has been highlighted in the earlier chapters of this book, both international and Islamic law seek to establish a global rules-based order where the security, safety, and the sanctity of human life and the welfare of citizens are of paramount importance. Although the definition of what "terrorism" is has evolved considerably since the events of 9/11, without common consensus, what is clear across the two realms is that the indiscriminate killing of innocents is categorically prohibited and universally condemned. At the heart of the two realms resides the principle of justice and proportionality in the acts that are undertaken to counter the threats posed by terrorism. Proactive responses to terrorism also find synergy between the sources of international and Islamic law.

Whereas it can be argued that the rules of international law have been construed and interpreted with an element of trepidation among international relations analysts, observing the reaction and response to the "war on terror" over the last two decades, there is no doubt that the ways in which the threat of terrorism have been approached will be universally condemned by both International Humanitarian Law (IHL) and Islamic law. The responses to the threat of terrorism across the globe may well have been different if checked by the ethics, principles, and norms of international Islamic law, where the barometer and threshold to react and intervene militarily in certain countries would be much higher, based on principles of certainty (*yaqeen*).

Treating Prisoners of War, Hostages according to Islamic International law and Public International law

When developing the Islamic Law of War in International Armed Conflicts, the Muslim jurists paid the greater part of their attention to the following issues: the protection of civilians and non-combatants; the protection of personal and military property, wherein the objective is achieving surrender; and the treatment of prisoners.

The Protection of Civilians and Non-Combatants

The Sources of Islamic Law guarantee the protection of civilians and non-combatants, stating that fighting on the battlefield must be directed solely against enemy combatants. Civilians and non-combatants must not be deliberately harmed during hostilities. This principle is clearly set out in the verse that states: "And fight in the way of God those who fight against you and do not transgress, indeed God does not like transgressors." Al-Rāzī (d. 1209) defines *al-muqātilın* (combatants), as he understood them, from this verse as follows:

> They must be taking part in the fighting; anyone who is willing or prepared to fight cannot be described as a combatant, except in metaphor, until they enter into combat.

Several of the Prophet's Hadiths specifically prohibit the targeting of women, children, the elderly, *'usafā'* and *ash āb al-sawa mi'* (monks or religious hermits). The word *'usafā'* is the plural of the word *'asıf*, which means hired man or employee, and in the context of war it refers to anyone who works for, or is paid by, the enemy to perform services on the battlefield, as was frequent practice in wars in the past. These individuals would perform tasks such as minding belongings and animals but would not engage in the fighting and therefore could not be classified as combatants.

The Companions who followed Prophet Muhammad's example; for instance, the first caliph Abu-Bakr (d. 634) instructed his army commander:

> Do not kill a child or a woman; or an aged person; do not cut down fruit-bearing trees or destroy buildings; do not slaughter a sheep or a camel except for food; do not burn or drown palm trees; do not loot; and do not be cowardly.[282]

Based on the distinction between combatants and non-combatants, Islamic jurists set out detailed provisions on two key methods of warfare that were used in the primitive wars described above: these are *al-tatarrus* (human shields) and *al-bayāt* (night attacks), both of which were first deliberated during the time of Prophet Muhammad.

With respect to bayāt, fighting at night meant that the two armies were unable to fight hand to hand because they could not see one another in the darkness; this rendered it necessary in such cases to target the enemy using mangonels or other types of indiscriminate weapons. On that basis, according to the Hadith narrated by Anas ibn Mālik, Prophet Muhammad avoided attacking the enemy at night.

Protection of Property

Through the study of the wars that took place between Muslims and their enemies during the lifetime of the Prophet, and the permissible weapons and methods of warfare as discussed above, it is clear that in Islam, war is not an indiscriminate free-for-all in which anyone and anything can be targeted. The use of military force is only permissible if required by military necessity, and the wanton destruction of enemy property is not covered by this condition; such acts instead constitute a crime of *"al-fasād* (destruction, damage) in the land." This position was advocated by Imam al-Awza 'ı (d. 774), who said that:

> it is prohibited for Muslims to commit any sort of takhrıb, wanton destruction, [during the course of hostilities] in enemy territories because that is fasād and God does not like fasād and referred to the following Qur'anic verse: "when he turns his back, he hastens about the earth, to do corruption there and to destroy the tillage and the stock." [283]

Military Property: The Objective is Surrender

It should also be noted that some jurists such as Al-Shafi'ī (d. 820) and Ibn Ḥazm (d. 1064) drew a distinction between inanimate objects and living property such as horses, cattle and bees, and ruled that inflicting damage on living property such as livestock for any reason other than for food was tantamount to torture, which is prohibited in Islam. Notwithstanding this, the jurists did permit the targeting of enemy horses when enemy warriors were fighting on horseback, because in this case the horse was being used as military equipment. All of these provisions are in line with Article 51 (4) of API, which prohibits indiscriminate attacks, which are defined as:

> (a) those which are not directed at a specific military objective; (b) those which employ a method or means of combat which cannot be directed at a specific military objective; or (c) those which employ a method or means of combat the effects of which cannot be limited as required by this Protocol;

and consequently, in each such case, are of a nature to strike military objectives and civilians or civilian objects without distinction.[284]

At the Battle of Badr in 624 CE, the first battle in Islamic history, the Muslims buried the corpses of all enemies killed. Furthermore, at the Battle of the Trench in 627 CE, when the enemies of the Muslims requested the return of the corpse of Nawfal ibn 'Abd Allah ibn al Mughırah in exchange for 10,000 dirhams, the Prophet ordered for the body to be returned and refused to accept the money. As well as respect for humanity and preservation of the dignity of the dead, another reason Muslims ensured the burial of enemy corpses was to prevent them from decomposing in the open. On that basis, Ibn Ḥazm (d. 1064) instructed Muslims to bury the bodies of their deceased enemies because if they did not, the bodies would rot and could be eaten by predatory animals; this would be tantamount to mutilation, which is forbidden in Islam. Article 17 of the Geneva Convention I (GC I) also stipulates that the parties to a conflict must first carry out a medical examination of corpses to verify the identity of the deceased, then bury the body according to the applicable religious rites if possible.

Treatment of Prisoners

The Islamic approach to the issue of prisoners of war reflects many features typical of the Islamic legal system and shows the vital need to reinterpret certain legal provisions in order to respond to the requirements of the modern age. Most of the rules on "prisoners of war" (PoWs) according to Islamic law were based on the treatment of prisoners in the battle of Badr in the second year of the Islamic calendar (624 CE). In addition, the term PoWs was used to refer only to male combatants, because the custom at the time was for women or children who were captured to be enslaved or exchanged for Muslim prisoners.[285] At the battle of Badr, the Muslims managed to capture seventy male enemy combatants; this posed a challenge for the nascent Islamic state, which had yet to establish legislation on the legal status of PoWs. The Prophet Muhammad therefore consulted his Companions on the issue. To solve the additional challenge of providing shelter for the seventy prisoners, since nowhere specific had been prepared for this purpose, some of the prisoners were held in the mosque and the rest were divided up to be housed with the Companions of the Prophet. The Prophet instructed that the prisoners should be treated well, saying: "Observe good treatment towards the prisoners."

Islamic jurists were split into three camps over the law on PoWs in Islam. In the first camp was Ibn 'Abbās (d. 668), 'Abd Allah ibn 'Umar (d. 693), al-Ḥasan al-Baṣrı (d. 728) and Sa'ıd ibn Jubayr (d. 714), who argued that the law on prisoners in Islam required them to be freed by "grace" or "ransom" according to the first of these texts. The second camp, made up of some of the Hanafī jurists, advocated that the head of state was entitled to either execute the prisoners or enslave them, according to what best served the public interest, while Al-Shaybānı, one of the great Hanafī jurists, deemed it permissible to exchange enemy prisoners. The remaining Hanafī jurists advocated that the head of state was entitled to release prisoners as long as they remained in the Islamic state and paid the *jizya* (the tax levied to exempt eligible males from conscription). According to the Hanafī jurists, prisoners should not be allowed to return to their country because they would strengthen the enemy. The third camp, comprised of the majority of Muslim jurists, including the Shāfi'ıs, the Malikıs and the Hanbalıs, as well as al- Awzā'ı (d. 774) and Sufyān al-Thawrı (d. 778), advocated that the head of state,[286] based on the tenets of Islamic law and international humanitarian law, was entitled to choose one of the following four options, depending on what he deemed to best serve the public interest; that is, to execute some or all of the prisoners, to enslave them, to set them free, or to exchange them for Muslim prisoners.[287]

The management of dead bodies is a matter of human dignity. This dignity a right bestowed by God, and this dignity must be protected whether a person is alive or dead. The Prophet's instructions, referred to above, to avoid deliberately injuring enemy combatants in the face,[288] epitomise the synergy between Islamic and international humanitarian law as a sign of respecting human dignity.

The disconnect between gross violations of IHL and Islamic law being committed in Muslim contexts, necessitates an examination of the causes underlying the perpetrators' behaviour. It also requires that a series of adequate measures be taken by all concerned parties, including Muslim scholars, governments, and civil society organisations. The following constitute some of the main reasons for these violations. The first reason is the wide gap between theory and practice. The second reason is a lack of research by modern Muslim scholars into the areas of Islamic law that govern state affairs, especially regarding governance systems, war, and international relations. This has to do with cultural and political factors relating to the structure of the modern state in Muslim countries, as discussed by Jean-Marie Henckaerts and Louise Doswald-Beck.[289] The third reason is the existence in many Muslim countries of weak civil society institutions that do not contribute to solving the problems of their societies. A brief examination of Muslim history will demonstrate that the Muslim world has witnessed amazing periods of scientific, creative advancement and enlightenment the legacy from which Western models and constructs reaped immense benefits.[290]

Powell argues that *ceteris paribus*, an Islamic Legal System whose legal systems are deeply infused with tenets of Islamic law are likely to gravitate toward international settlement venues that resemble traditional Islamic law: these include third-party non-binding methods, such as conciliation and mediation. In contrast, ILS whose domestic legal systems embrace secular features are more receptive to international legal mechanisms, namely, arbitration and adjudication.[291]

Arbitration and adjudication, the two binding third-party mechanisms, constitute legal means of settling disputes according to international law, with disputants agreeing in advance to accept the award (arbitration) or judgement (adjudication). Both methods are based on relatively formal procedures of settlement, although rules of arbitration are more flexible than those of adjudication.[292]

International law offers states various methods for dispute settlement, with negotiations and adjudication constituting two opposites. The non-binding third-party methods sit in between these two extremities. Alternate legal designs of the different venues coexist, interact, and relate to states' domestic legal systems. After all, any form of dispute resolution is fundamentally based on a consideration of norms, principles, and rules.[293]

Law as played out in the Islamic courtroom—or for that matter, outside it—has a distinctive role. Only some international conflict management mechanisms suite certain ILS.[294] International adjudication is, in a sense, an interpretive exercise whereby judges decipher which rival norms should be applied to a case at hand: "when seeking to overturn all but the most flagrantly illegal state actions, litigants and courts must inevitably appeal to particular interpretations of such ambiguities [ambiguities between norms]."[295]

For international law, universalisation means borrowing and adapting concepts and principles from different legal traditions. Some scholars argue that to increase the predictability of the final settlement, states prefer to use resolution methods that resemble their domestic legal institutions simply because these methods are more familiar.[296]

Powell points out that because the Islamic realm has, by and large, not participated in the creation of these venues, and because most international judges are trained in the West, ILS have scant opportunity to embed elements of Shari'a into these mechanisms. Judge Abdulqawi Yusuf of the ICJ addressed this issue directly by stating that:

"In the 19th century, European states, which happened to be the most powerful nations during that period of human history, formed themselves into a sort of club of 'founders' which arrogated to itself the right to admit other members to the family of nations to whom international law would be applicable." [297]

Islamic influences are simply non-existent in arbitration and adjudication, both of which have been institutionally expressed almost exclusively in values inscribed within Western legal traditions.[298]

Powell makes the point, regarding her interviews with a state advocate, where the perceived impression was that the presence of Islamic legal arguments in international courts or arbitration tribunals depends almost entirely on the personal interests of judges or arbiters, who might simply be curious about Shari'a. In the advocate's words:

Lawyers like me are Western educated, but my interest in Islamic law is not because of my education but purely because of my personal interests. I have a huge library in Islamic law as if I am a geek, whereas other lawyers have no idea about those things. It is not because it's their fault, but because they are brought up in modern legal systems. They talk about it as if Islamic law provides answers, since they have been brought up to accept that there is Qur'an as the word of God and hadith. They get the basics, but they don't know the details.[299]

Islamic dispute resolution is one of the most powerful tools that one can apply when talking about Islam. Everything is ordained by God, and, to that extent, human agency is really limited. People will always find a way of ensuring that problems are resolved in a way and manner that helps the community grow.

As Hashmi writes, in the context of relations between states:

> "True peace (salaam) is therefore not merely an absence of war; it is the elimination of the grounds for strife or conflict, and the resulting waste and corruption (*fasad*) they create. Peace, not war or violence, is God's true purpose for humanity."[300]

Interestingly, the notion of justice lay at the centre of Jordanian King Abdullah II's 2006 speech at the ICJ:

> "Indeed, for Muslims, global good citizenship—justice and integrity in the dealings among people, regardless of faith, race or nationality—is a cornerstone of a righteous life. In the Qur'an it is written: 'Be just—that is closer to piety.'"[301]

While European and American litigation models are inherently based on a winner/loser dichotomy as well as legalistic and rational argumentation, the Islamic concept of settlement relies on a myriad of extra-legal values such as communal benefits, societal needs, and religion. There is thus a focus on the interests and needs of the community and society at large under Islamic law, rather than the primacy that is normally accorded to the individual. In the West, these notions lie outside the realm of law and legality, and do not fit neatly into the state's conception of a legitimate and unbiased dispute resolution process. In a sense, the Islamic way of conflict management is more receptive to intangible outcomes, outcomes that go beyond individual rights, gains or losses, and outcomes that affect the larger community. [302]

As Aida Othman explained to Powell:

> And if you assert a litigious culture in any way instead of going to the leader of the village and getting to sort out things for them, it just goes against the grain of the community. You will not be able to achieve this communal atmosphere: these people have weddings to organise, funerals to deal with together. Going to court cannot smooth out disagreements. You cannot have smooth operations through life when somebody goes and starts an action at the high court in the nearest town. It just does not work that way.[303]

The avoidance of legal proceedings is much more deeply ingrained in Islam than it is in the West.

An old Islamic maxim teaches *al-Sulh seyed al-ahkam*, that mediation/reconciliation is the superior rule. *Sulh*, a concept that undergirds the Islamic paradigm of dispute resolution, roughly translates to compromise of action, conciliation, or an amicable settlement. Informality was deeply engrained in the fabric of Arab tribal societies and certainly predates the rise of Islam. A ruler, a healer, or an influential nobleman often took on the role of intermediary in intratribal disagreements.[304] The Qur'an embraces this philosophy of reconciliation: "There is no blame on them if they arrange an amicable settlement between themselves, and such settlement is best." *Sulh* was the Prophet's favoured method of dispute resolution. In fact, the Prophet's personally mediated conflicts between his close followers and between clan members.[305]

Key methods of dispute resolution involve arbitration by a third party knowledgeable in Islamic law, and *qada*, adjudication by qadi based on Shari'a. Unlike *sulh*, an arbitrator and a qadi have the power to impose their decision on the disputants and play a more institutionalised role in the proceedings. Both *tahkim* and *qada* are based on the parties subjecting themselves to a verdict of an intermediary who is knowledgeable in Islamic law. *Sulh*, however, can be incorporated within the framework of adjudication. A judge who is to embrace his role as a mediator and a conciliator can encourage the parties to seek mediation before the commencement of the trial.[306]

Illuminating examples of informal dispute resolution include Jirga and Shura in Afghanistan, both of which embrace restorative informal justice and societal harmony. Shura is a local gathering, or a local court universally understood, and Jirga is an ad hoc council made up of local elders and important male figures who make consultative and often final decisions about a wide range of issues.

International Legal System (ILS) and International Peaceful Resolution Methods

Mediation and conciliation entail an ongoing dialogue between the disputant and the intermediary. Goertz et al argue, "Mediators have the freedom to offer suggestions, construct solutions, or change the payoffs (through use of selective incentives or punishments) for all tentative outcomes."[307]

The international process of mediation and reconciliation has less inconsistency and flows naturally from the entire resolution process. The no winner or loser principle in Arab society is an important one when it comes to high stake disputes.

As the Jan Mayen conciliation commission declared:

"The Conciliation Commission shall not act as a court of law. Its function is to make recommendation to the two governments which in the unanimous opinion of the commission will lead to acceptable and equitable solution of the problems involved. If a dispute centres on a question of facts, employing international law may be unnecessary."[308]

Hashmi states that "The issues of war and peace thus fall within the purview of divine legislation for humanity."[309]

Islamic Collectives and Just Ordered Community

Al Fadl states that "the Qur'an is revealed over a period of Twenty-One years and carries fundamental weight in all aspects of life, including the peaceful resolution of disputes."[310] Sachedina asserts that:

When law and faith merge in an individual's life, they create a sense of security and integrity about the great responsibility of pursuing justice for its own sake. And when this sense of security and integrity is projected to the collective life of the community, it conduces to social harmony. Peace, then, is belief translated into action.[311]

There are multiple declarations and charters such as the OIC Charter objectives, the Arab Charter of Human Rights, and the Cairo Declaration which can all be used as sources for conflict resolution, peace, and reconciliation. Islamic Legal System is in essence citizens expectations about the role of Sharia in public life.

The way Islamic law and secular law feature and intertwine in ILS's domestic legal systems shape these states' attitudes toward international law and international settlement venues. These attitudes are visible because ILS makes choices regarding conflict management venues when they are involved in disputes. In addition, the ILS could accept the jurisdiction of the ICJ. Some of these states choose to recognise its adjudicatory powers, and some shy away from the Court. ILS do not all sing from the same hymn sheet and do not project uniform norms onto the international arena.[312]

Dialogue and Diplomacy based on Islamic Humanitarian Law and International Humanitarian Law

The importance of the role of dialogue and diplomatic tact cannot be underestimated when it comes to peaceful reconciliation. It is for this reason that the governance structures in both Western nation states and Muslim states are based on models where the various divisions, offices, attaches, secretariats are either ingrained in their evolutionary progress or created to deal with contemporary geo-political challenges.

To facilitate the above, nation states in both the West and Muslim lands have departments of foreign affairs, defence, security, justice, and so on, where power is delegated to senior politicians, officers, and statespersons. Intertwined in the above rubric are the interlocutors who will be given the authority on behalf the state or, in some cases non-state actors, to partake in the dialogue process to help resolve disputes.

The importance of dialogue and diplomacy resides at the heart of Islamic and international humanitarian law. Without this important pillar, it is virtually impossible for disputing parties to come to a collective agreement in a conflict situation, and for it to be resolved in a peaceful manner. The authority and power that is either directly represented in the dialogue and diplomatic tract by the heads of state, or those to whom it has been delegated on behalf of the state, is equally crucial here. Principles of trust are also of great importance to ensure that whatever agreements are made are honoured. Intertwined in this process is also the role of international organisations such as the UN, the European Union, and other supra-national bodies that provide leverage to steer the negotiations to a peaceful outcome.

Use of Force According to Public and Islamic International Law

A final topic to briefly consider is the issue of 'use of force'. On Use of Force, Dawoody points out that the impact of Armed Conflicts, including Non-International Armed Conflicts (NIACs), is no longer local or regional, but global. In that regard, a reported eighty per cent of the humanitarian crises currently afflicting humankind are attributable to armed conflicts.[313] We must therefore think of the issue as one with truly global dimensions.

On that basis, greater efforts are needed to enforce the provisions of international law across regions and nations. This statement also reaffirms the aforementioned notion that the laws of Islam are binding, regardless of the conduct of the enemy, and that reciprocity does not justify criminal acts. It is imperative to use international humanitarian law (IHL), but also to do everything possible to prevent the occurrence of armed conflicts in the first place, and then, once conflicts have ended, to take the necessary measures to ensure that post-conflict justice is carried out to prevent those conflicts from re-igniting.

It is widely acknowledged that respect for IHL is important owing to its capacity to reduce the scale of destruction, or to introduce a degree of humanity into situations of armed conflict, where acts of brutality, barbarity, and destruction occur. Therefore, it is especially important to study the primary sources on the Islamic laws of war, because of the significant and tangible role they play in influencing the behaviour of the warring parties who use its provisions to justify their acts of hostility. IHL limits devastation and destruction.

Human Rights and Humanitarians According to Public and International Islamic Law

It is important to state that in contemporary international law, human rights play a fundamental role, as encapsulated and enshrined in various international treaties, conventions, customary sources, and international bodies. The interface between human rights and principles of humanitarianism, public international law, and the core tenets of international Islamic law, epitomise the broad avenues for alignment between these supra-national legal frameworks of the international rules-based order. Among the multitude of human rights and obligations that an individual enjoys under these supra-national frameworks, at its core resides the fundamental human right and sanctity of life, which is immutable.

What this chapter has demonstrated is that there is a significant synergy between principles of international humanitarian law and international Islamic humanitarian law in the areas of conflict resolution, arbitration, peace and reconciliation, encapsulated and enshrined in the sources of these global jurisprudential models. Juxtaposing these models against each other is thus a very illuminating exercise.

References

al-Dawoody, Ahmed. "Islamic law and International Humanitarian Law: An Introduction to the main principles." *International Review of the Red Cross*, 99, no. 3 (2017): 995–1018

Al Ghunami, Mohammad Talat, *The Muslim Conception of International Law and the Western Approach*, The Hague, the Netherlands, 1968, 95.

Antonio Casesse, *International Law*, Second Edition, Oxford University Press, 2005.

An-Nai'im, Abdullahi Ahmed, *Islam and the Secular State: Negotiating the Future of Shari'a*. Cambridge, MA: Harvard University Press, 2008.

Badr, Gamal Moursi, *A Survey of Islamic International Law, Proceedings of the Annual Meeting,* American Society of International Law, 76 (April 22-24): 55-61.

Bassiouni M. Cherif, *The Shari'a and Islamic Criminal Justice in Time of War and Peace*, New York, Cambridge University Press, 2014.

Brierly, James I. *The Law of Nations: An Introduction to the International Law of Peace,* Sixth Edition, Edited by Sir Humphrey Waldock, Oxford University Press, 1963.

Clapham, A. "Brierly's Law of Nations, Seventh Edition, Oxford University Press, 2012.

Christine Chinkin and Mary Kaldor, *International Law And New Wars,* Cambridge University Press, 2017.

Cole, Juan. "Muhammad and Justinian: Roman Legal Traditions and the Qurʾān." *Journal of Near Eastern Studies* 79 no. 2 (2020): 183–96.

Conciliation Commission on the Continental Shelf area between Iceland and Jan Mayen: Report and recommendations to the governments of Iceland and Norway, decision of June 1981, Volume XXVII, 1-34. (Accessed January 2, 2021).

David Armstrong, Theo Farrell and Helen Lambert, *International Law and International Relations,* Second Edition, Cambridge University Press, 2012.

Dicey, Albert Venn. *Lectures Introductory to the Study of the Law of the Constitution*. No. 43445-43449. London: Macmillan, 1885.

El Fadl, Khaled Abou. *"Islam and the Theology of Power." Middle East Report* 221 (2001): 28–33.

El Fadl, Khaled Abou. *"The Rules of Killing at War: An Inquiry into Classical Sources." The Muslim World* 89/2 (April 1999): 144–57.

El Fadl, Khaled Abou, *Conflict Resolution as a Normative Value in Islamic Law: Handling Disputes with Non-Muslims."* In Douglas Johnson, ed., *Faith Based Diplomacy: Trumping Realpolitik,* Oxford, UK: Oxford University Press, 2003, 178-209.

Goertz, Gary, Paul F. Diehl, and Alexandru Balas, *The Evolution of Peace in International System, Oxford, Oxford University Press, 2016.*

Grotius, Hugo. *On the Law of War and Peace.* Cambridge: Cambridge University Press, 2012.

Hallaq, Wael B. 2009b. *Sharia: Theory Practice Transformations,* Cambridge, UK, Cambridge University Press.

Hashmi, Sohail H. *"Saving and Taking Life in War: Three Modern Muslim Views." The Muslim World* 89/2 (1999): 158–80.

Hashmi, Sohail H, *Islamic Ethics in International Society.* In Sohail H. Hashmi, ed, *Islamic Political Ethics: Civil Society, Pluralism, and Conflict, Princeton, Princeton University Press, 2002, 194-217.*

Henckaerts, Jean-Marie, and Louise Doswald-Beck, eds. *Customary International Humanitarian Law, Vol. 1: Rules*. Cambridge: Cambridge University Press, 2005, https://www.icrc.org/en/doc/assets/files/other/customary-international-humanitarian-law-i-icrc-eng.pdf (Accessed 12th March, 2022)

Ḥammıdulla h, Muḥammad. *Muslim Conduct of State: Being a Treatise on Siyar, That is Islamic Notion of Public International Law, Consisting of the Laws of Peace, War and Neutrality, Together with Precedents from Orthodox Practice and Preceded by a Historical and General Introduction*, rev. and enl. 5th ed. Sh. Muhammad Ashraf, Lahore, 1968.

Hillier, Tim. *Sourcebook on Public International Law*. London: Routledge, 1998.

International Committee of the Red Cross. "Protection of the Civilian Population." https://www.icrc.org/en/doc/what-we-do/protecting-civilians/overview-protection-civilian-population.htm (Accessed 12th March, 2022)

International Court of Justice. *Statute of the International Court of Justice*, https://www.icj-cij.org/en/statute (Accessed 12th March, 2022)

Leslie C. Green, *The Contemporary Law of Armed Conflict*, Melland Schill Studies in International Law, Third Edition, Manchester University Press, 2014.

Lionel Giles, *The Art of War, by Sun Tzu*, The Project Gutenberg eBook, May 1994 (updated December 28, 2005), The Art of War (utoledo.edu) (accessed January 1, 2022)

Maldives, Republic of. *Constitution of the Maldives* (2008), https://www.constituteproject.org/constitution/Maldives_2008?lang=en (Accessed 13th March, 2022)

Mayer, A. E. "War and Peace in the Islamic Tradition and International Law." In *Just War and Jihad: Historical and Theoretical Perspectives on War and Peace in Western and Islamic Traditions*, edited by J. T. Johnson and J. Kelsay, 195–226. Westport: Greenwood Press, 1991.

Peters, Rudolph F. *Jihad in Classical and Modern Islam*. Princeton, NJ: Markus Wiener, 1996.

Powell, E.J. *Islamic Law and International Law: Peaceful Resolution of Disputes*. Oxford: Oxford University Press, 2020.

Rosen, Lawrence, *The Justice of Islam,* Oxford, UK; Oxford University Press, 2000.

Remarks by His Majesty King Abdullah II at the International Court of Justice, Royal Hashemite Court, King Abdullah II Official Website, October 31, 2006. Remarks by His Majesty King Abdullah II At the International Court of Justice | Royal Hashemite Court (rhc.jo) (Accessed January 2, 2021).

Sachedina, Abdul Aziz, *The Islamic Roots of Democratic Pluralism*, Oxford, Oxford University Press, 2011.

Salaymeh, Lena. "Early Islamic Legal-Historical Precedents: Prisoners of War," *Law and History Review* 26, no. 3 (2008): 521–544.

Shaw, Malcolm N. *International Law*, Cambridge, UK, Cambridge University Press, 2003.

Sheikh Wahbeh al-Zuhli, *Islam and International Law, Vol 87, No. 858, June 2005, 278.* Islam and international law (icrc.org) (Accessed January 3, 2022).
Shuaib, Farid, *The Islamic Legal System in Malaysia*, Pacific Rim Law and Policy Journal, 21 (1), 2012, 85-113.

Vienna Convention on the Law of Treaties 1969, Treaties Conflicting with a peremptory norm of general international law ("jus cogens"), Vienna Convention on the Law of Treaties (1969) (un.org) (Accessed January 3, 2022).

Weiss, Bernard G, *The Spirit of Islamic Law*, Athens, University of Georgia Press, 2006.

Yusuf Abdulaqawi, *Diversity of Legal Traditions and International Law: Keynote Address, Cambridge Journal of International and Comparative Law*, 2 (4), 2013; 681-703.

Chapter Four

Peace and Reconciliation in Practice

Abstract

Thus far, we have examined in detail multiple sources of public international law, customary norms, human rights, and theology through the lens of Islamic law. We have analysed the several focal points wherein international and Islamic law clearly converge, and the core points of divergence between these two canons. In this chapter, this comparative and theoretical analysis will be *applied* to case studies from across the world. It is only by locating theoretical findings in the context of practical conflict and disputes that we can make sense of how Islamic law can shape discourses on peace and reconciliation.

This chapter focuses on current theatres of conflict around the world, such as Afghanistan, Kashmir, and Palestine–Israel. These sites of conflict are chosen because of their deep geo-political ramifications on prominent regions across the world, namely South Asia and the Middle East. Moreover, Islam plays a crucial role in each of these conflicts, and thus a discussion of Islamic law and conflict resolution in these contexts is fitting and, indeed, timely.

Through a close study of these three sites of conflict and a critical discussion of peacebuilding in these contexts, this chapter discusses how the confluence between Islamic law and international law can help to shape discourses towards peace and reconciliation. The chapter begins with a case study of Afghanistan, then proceeds to a case study of Palestine and Israel and concludes with a case study of Kashmir. In all three sections of the chapter, I shall discuss how core principles of Islamic law can inform and strengthen peacebuilding and conflict resolution in conjunction with international law in these crucial regions.

Afghanistan

At the time of writing this book, the global spotlight has turned its attention to the situation in Afghanistan. In 2021, the Taliban rapidly assumed control over the country after a Western occupation that had lasted for more than 20 years. In the course of its history as a nation, Afghanistan has been subjugated to multiple phases of occupation, dating back to the nineteenth century, when Britain, looking to protect its Indian empire from Russia, engaged in a series of British–Afghan wars (1838–42, 1878–80, 1919–21).[314] Noted for being the "Graveyard of Empires," Afghanistan has been the epicentre of conflict for many decades. Numerous stakeholders around the world have attempted to lay claim to parts of Afghanistan based on their geo-political, economic, or military interests.

The first manifestation of the Taliban came to the fore in 1995, with the revived iteration (commonly termed Taliban 2.0) returning to the fore in 2021. The Taliban reclaimed the land after US President Joe Biden announced a formal date for the withdrawal of US troops on August 30, 2021. Considering the control that the Taliban has today, and the history of conflict within Afghanistan, it is important to examine how peacebuilding and conflict-resolution processes have played out in the region. Drawing critical links between Islamic law and international law, this section will analyse how peace and reconciliation processes work in *practice* in the region of Afghanistan.

During the period between 9/11 and the present day, there have been numerous opportunities to broker a peaceful resolution to the conflict. If we are to understand the processes of peacebuilding in Afghanistan, we must first delve briefly into the history of the Taliban as it exists today.

The Taliban of 2021 did not emerge from a vacuum. Rather, it is a product of complex international and internal factors. The ideology of the Taliban can be traced back to a religious seminary in India, the Darul Uloom Deoband, which was founded in 1866. Its core teachings include the belief that by returning to the core principles of Islam, Indian Muslims could resist British rule. Many of the Taliban leadership underwent training at Deobandi seminaries. Some would argue that the current Taliban movement that has emerged in Afghanistan (with offshoots in Pakistan) has diverged from the teachings and principles of the Indian Deobandi ideology and has subsequently orientated itself towards the ideology of Wahhabism. This belief system is based on a rigid, reformist understanding and application of Islamic law, and traces its roots to its founder, Muhammad ibn Abd al Wahhab (1703–1792). A key theological difference between the two reformist movements is that Wahhabism disregards the various schools of Islamic law that form a crucial component and corpus of the Islamic tradition, and instead favours a more literalistic interpretation, application, and orientation of Islam using the Qur'an and hadith as the core sources.

The claim that the Taliban governs by the *principles of Islamic law* has been contested by many scholars.[315] Scholars often allege that the correct interpretation of the tenets of the Islamic tradition finds no reflection in the Taliban. Instead, the Taliban follow a rigid interpretation of Islamic law— one that shows its core principles in a poor light. Owing to this, Western observers have critiqued the Taliban's ideology (wrongly attributed to the core tenets of Islamic law) as draconian and even as anathema to the principles valued by the West, such as peace, freedom and democracy.

The relationship between Afghanistan and the West has played out on the global stage as a conflict between Western ideals and the religious ideals of Islam. The renowned Afghan Islamic academic and Professor, Mohammad Hashim Kamali, shared his reflections on Afghanistan in an interview conducted twenty years after the 9/11 attacks on the Twin Towers:

> The background of the September 11 attacks is the post-colonial dialectic between Western excesses and Muslim reactions, the latter taking the form of Islamic fundamentalism and Islamic resurgence. And this story tends to repeat itself. The attacks occurred as a consequence of Muslim resentment. The Western counter-response was the war in Afghanistan, but it was totally misplaced and disproportionate, with manifold destruction and thousands of bombings and killings every night. And the same thing occurred in Iraq.[316]

The West's negative attitude towards Islam and the narrative that the Taliban in Afghanistan is an exclusive fundamentalist *Islamic* organisation portraying the depiction of Islam is contested as unfair and inaccurate based on the normative tents of the *Islamic* tradition. As discussed in the preceding chapters, the core principles of Islamic law in fact highlight *the importance of peace*. They are antithetical to much of the project that the Taliban espouses on the ground. In order, then, to understand how Islamic law and its core tenets can inform the conflict in Afghanistan *towards* peacebuilding, we must first take a closer look at the role of Islam in Afghanistan's domestic legal system.

In the report *Islamic Law, Customary Law, and Afghan Informal Justice*, the author Hamid M. Khan notes that "Afghanistan's legal system has drawn on a mix of customary tribal law, primarily derived from the Pashtun community's code of Pashtunwali, and Islamic legal traditions valued for their universal and unifying characteristics."[317] We see that the domestic legal system is often based on Islamic legal principles and draws heavily from the tradition. Take for instance the 2004 Constitution of Afghanistan, which is significantly rooted in Islamic law. Article 130 of the Constitution states that if there are no clear constitutional provisions or laws that are applicable to a particular case at hand, the courts of law shall seek justice in the "spirit of Hanafi jurisprudence."[318] Note that in legal systems in the West as well, courts are often directed to rely on principles of equity when there are no clear legal rules applicable to case—that is, when the "law runs out." The difference here seems to be that instead of relying on perceivably secular principles—such as that of equity—the 2004 Constitution draws explicitly from Hanafi jurisprudence to resolve disputes when the law runs out.[319]

Furthermore, the Constitution of Afghanistan has explicitly religious elements and encourages the practice of Islamic legal traditions through a state-sanctioned religious education system for all. This emphasis on education through principles of *shari'a* as interpreted by the state has been a constant feature across different constitutions in Afghanistan. Consider Article 22 of the 1931 Constitution, which stated:

> In order to make sure that all educational institutions conduct their programs in accordance with Islamic principles, all educational institutions shall be monitored and inspected by the Afghanistan Islamic government.[320]

In more recent material, we can turn to Article 45 of Afghanistan's 2004 Constitution, which states:

> The state shall devise and implement a unified educational curriculum based on the tenets of the sacred religion of Islam, national culture as well as academic principles, and develop religious curricula for schools on the basis of existing Islamic sects in Afghanistan.[321]

Even in the realm of court procedures, Supreme Court judges in Afghanistan are often required to take "holy oaths."[322] Principles and tenets from Islamic law are thus central to the domestic legal system in Afghanistan.

However, despite popular conceptions that Islamic law holds a supreme legal status, field surveys indicate that, *in practice*, its core principles and provisions are often disregarded in favour of customary law that is intended to maintain community consensus. If we examine the distinction between Islamic law and customary law in this sense, one sees that the latter is often laden with unjust practices and connotations that the former explicitly condemns. As Hashmi notes:

> "When people form social units, they become all the more prone to disobey God's laws through the obstinate persistence in wrongdoing caused by custom and social pressures" (2:13-14, 37:69, 43:22).[323]

It is thus the customs and prevalent social inequities caused by conflict that sometimes allow the internal legal system in Afghanistan to be prone to strife. Islamic law is not the basis for this, but rather is—and can be—the antidote to unjust customary practices.

This is further evident in the realm of women's rights. A particular concern in Afghanistan is the structural marginalisation of women in society. Women suffer from a violation of their rights, violence, discrimination, and abuse in the region.[324] Media and news outlets across the world report about the poor treatment and status of women in Afghanistan. As Amnesty International UK noted when speaking to interlocuters who have lived in Afghanistan, "Afghan women were the ones who lost most from the war and militarisation."[325] The gendered dimension of the conflict in the region and its impact on the lives of women is thus an inescapable reality.

While women in Afghanistan are indeed suffering from an overarching and concerning denial of rights, this is attributable to injustices and biases rooted in *customary practice* rather than in formal legal norms. An analysis of the legal material in Afghanistan shows that women are accorded several rights and protections that are laid down in a range of legal texts, conventions, and practices. The problem does not stem from the laws itself then, but rather from their uncharitable interpretation with regard to further customary norms. Let us take a closer look.

The laws of Afghanistan formally vest women with a range of significant rights. For instance, Article 22 of the 2004 constitution extends equality to both men and women.[326] Women are given the right to own and inherit property under the Article 70 of the Afghan Civil Code, 1977.[327] Article 71 further sets a minimum age for marriage in the region to protect Afghan women from early marriages and child marriages—practices that are prevalent in the region.[328] Furthermore, the rights of women to choose their partners is also protected under the Afghan Criminal Code (1979), in which there are codified protections for eloped couples and a distinction is created between elopement and kidnapping.[329] Within the public sphere, the laws on election in Afghanistan protect women's right to vote and also provide affirmative action policies to secure seats for women in elected bodies.[330] In addition to this, women have a right to guaranteed legal aid and a range of policy measures and schemes—such as the Afghanistan National Development Strategy (2008) and the National Action Plan for Women of Afghanistan (2008)—emphasise the importance of gender equality in both the private and the public spheres of society in Afghanistan. On paper, then, women's rights seem to be well-protected by the legal system in the region.

However, these formal measures have only occasionally translated into substantive equality in practice. As the United States Institute of Peace notes in Special Report 347, despite certain advancements for women at the ground level (mostly in the sphere of education and leadership), severe gender-based injustices persist. The report states:

> Despite the ban on child marriage, the Afghan Ministry of Public Health estimates that 21 percent of all women were married by age fifteen and another 53 percent by age eighteen. Women still face barriers in accessing education, which hinders their access to public life. Despite the declared goal that women fill at least 30 percent of civil servant positions, women are routinely excluded from civil service hiring, or when hired are denied promotion. Female victims of sexual violence and trafficking are frequently persecuted and incarcerated for moral crimes, and their predators are only infrequently indicted or incarcerated. In other words, despite formal guarantees, the courts and society at large still act within the framework of conservative social norms that restrict women's rights in economic and political spheres.[331]

What causes this discrepancy between law and practice? On critical examination, it becomes apparent that Islamic law—as understood in the context of Afghanistan—has emphasised and protected the rights of women. It is due to a range of customary practices that lack any religious sanction that gender-based injustices persist in the region. The way forward for women's rights groups has thus been to speak of gender-based justice and rights *through* the framework of Islamic law. This can be done only within the folds of Islamic law—where legal interpretations of the relevant texts are developed in order to further the aims of women's rights and gender-based equality.

Special Report 347 notes that there have been such programmes in Afghanistan that seek to *interpret* principles of Islamic law in order to achieve women's rights and emancipation. The Report states:

> "The biggest legal-literacy project applying sharia-based principles in Afghanistan was funded by USAID and implemented by Checchi Consulting. This program, which began in 2010 and ran through February 2014, educated traditional dispute resolution forums on provisions of Afghan law and taught the basics of Islamic law. Women's rights under Afghan law were explained by providing parallel provisions within Islamic law, illustrating concepts using quotes from the Quran and the Sunnah."[332]

Initiatives such as this take an *internal perspective* to gender empowerment and use the tools that have been discussed in this book—cardinal principles of Islamic law—to fight for women's rights. Initiatives along these lines seem to be the need of the hour in Afghanistan.

One objection that could be levied against my argument—which seeks an internal reimagination of Islamic law along principles of equality, justice, and fairness—would be that this compromises the 'core character' of the religious scriptures in Islamic law. However, there is a distinction at play here between text and interpretation. As Ziba Mir-Hosseini argues, there is an important difference to be drawn between law as scriptures and law as practice, which can be translated into a distinction between Shari'a law and *fiqh*. Hosseini writes:

> In Muslim belief, Shari'a—revealed law, literally "the way"—is the totality of God's Will as revealed to the Prophet Muhammad. *Fiqh*—the science of jurisprudence, literally "understanding"—is the process of human endeavour to discern and extract legal rules from the sacred sources of Islam— that is, the Qur'an and the Sunnah (the practice of the Prophet, as contained in hadith, traditions). In other words, while the Shari'a is sacred, universal, and eternal, *fiqh* is human and—like any other system of jurisprudence— subject to change ... *Fiqh* texts, which are patriarchal in both spirit and form, are frequently invoked as God's law, as a means to silence and frustrate Muslims' search for legal justice and equality, which are intrinsic to this-worldly justice.[333]

I suggest, therefore, that we must draw distinctions between the transcendental realm of *Shari'a* and the human, fallible realm of *fiqh*. The former, as Hosseini writes:

> "Condemns all relations of exploitation and domination, underpins Muslim women's quest and the critique of patriarchal constructions of gender relations, which are to be found not only in the vast corpus of jurisprudential texts but also in the positive laws that are claimed to be rooted in the sacred texts." [334]

The latter is the human understanding of the divine will—and thus is often mired in gender-based inequality and injustice.

An understanding of Islamic law and the distinction between sacred Shari'a texts and *fiqh* reveals helps secure the goals of women empowerment and humanitarian goals in the region. We can better identify the problem—and thereby challenge it—as being a problem of *interpretation* of human understandings that are rooted in customary social practices rather than religious texts itself. This warns against tainting all of Islam because, indeed, the religious Islamic law texts are committed deeply to peace and equality. It correctly identifies *fiqh* or the practice and interpretations of Islamic law as often leading to inequality and injustice.

Moving beyond the realm of women's issues, we see that this focus on the critical interpretations of Islamic legal texts to introduce just social practice is important in other areas as well. For instance, to bring in an issue central to international law and policy, we see that Islamic law can interact closely with international law in *resolving violent disputes*. Khan places particular importance on the rule of law in resolving violent conflict situations.[335] As noted in the preceding chapter, the 1980 Constitution of Afghanistan declared that "the Democratic Republic of Afghanistan will make efforts on the basis of good intentions and the principle of peaceful co-existence to help resolve justly and peacefully all the existing unsettled problems among neighbouring countries in the region."[336] The notion of peaceful settlement—a central tenet in Islamic law—thus finds mention in legal historical texts in Afghanistan. With this in mind, it has often been advised that disputing parties must adopt modes of dispute resolution that are not solely adversarial. This has been emphasised a great deal in Islamic law.

The spirit of dispute resolution can be seen clearly because many counties have entered in negotiations with Afghanistan's ruling groups, and even with the Taliban, which continues to have control over Afghanistan. The countries that have been involved in negotiations with the Taliban include the U.S., Russia, Pakistan, Qatar, Afghanistan and—in recent years—India and China. Qatar has been deemed a "neutral" venue to host most of the negotiations in Doha, where the Taliban also have an office. Intertwined in the various diplomatic tracts are the key interlocutors, who play a pivotal role in helping to broker a peaceful resolution to the conflict. This reflects the importance of peaceful settlement of disputes in Afghanistan - a principle that, we have seen, is fundamentally enshrined under Islamic law.

Another core component that has synergy in international and Islamic law is that of the rights of minorities. Under Islamic law, one issue that is oft discussed is the legal treatment of religious minorities—in particular, non-Muslim minorities who live and permanently reside in Muslim nations or polities. These minorities are often known as the *dhimmis*.[337] The *dhimmis* were given rights and protections under Islamic laws and the spirit of harmony was supposed to be prevalent in the treatment of religious minorities. In Afghanistan, Islamic law was infused in the domestic legal order in such a way that the rights of minorities were protected. As Julia Schiwal, a historian of Afghanistan, highlights:

> Since the constitution of 1923's creation and subsequent modification in 1926, there has been no constitution in Afghanistan from 1923–1991 that did not afford some religious protections to religious minorities. Furthermore,

these protections frequently established free practice of religion in the same sentences or paragraphs that they clearly state the government was a Muslim one. Textually, Muslim identity and religious freedom were tied together. The 2004 constitution of Afghanistan provided protections to religious minorities and women as well, while also establishing the Muslim character of the state.[338]

While these protections exist at the stage of the laws, this must translate more clearly into practice—wherein religious minorities are protected from violence and discrimination in Afghanistan. As part of the conflict resolution, peace, and reconciliation process between differing groups in Afghanistan, it is important that the core human rights principles of equality and citizenship for the different groups are upheld. We must note that even the law of the land in Afghanistan—informed by principles of Islam—is committed to the protection of the rights of minorities. While there is a clear and overarching idea that "Islam is the sacred religion of Afghanistan," Article 2 of the 2004 constitution also states that followers of other religions are free to exercise their faith and perform their religious rites within the limits of the law.[339] There is thus a clear indication that the religious freedom of minorities must be protected and that communities from different groups should co-exist in harmony.

It is through a combination of these core principles of Islamic law—interpreted through values such as justice, equity, and fairness that international law discourse holds valuable—we can see that several issues on the ground in Afghanistan can find better and more peaceful resolution. Studies indicate that if change and progress is to be brought about in Afghanistan, discussions of values in "secular" terms or couched in Western ideals is not very effective.[340] Instead, it is necessary to draw from the rich tradition of Islamic law so that this may resonate with the masses in Afghanistan and act as a catalyst for change.

Professor Akbar Ahmed points out that the principles of justice and compassion can be used as tools to broker peaceful outcomes to conflict.[341] However, there is a caveat to this as Islamic Law, in its pristine holistic form, is not implemented and fully functional in any state around the world. Professor Ahmed, who has a more than three decades of experience in the Civil Service of Pakistan (where his posts included Commissioner in Balochistan and Political Agent in the Tribal areas including Waziristan) provides an example of the tenure of the Wali of Swat, post Pakistan independence in 1947, where principles of Islamic law based on justice and compassion were in force. The key facets that enabled this to function were based on a strong ruler who had authority and force to back it up.[342] It was also not an exclusive religious legal model but a mixture of some Islamic law, Swat state law, Civil and Criminal Law, Tribal Law, and often a poor man in Swat would not know what law he was being adjudicated on. Professor Ahmed was adamant to explain that it important to not to conflate the example in Swat with the Jirga system in Afghanistan. The Jirga system based on the Council of Elders is effective when operating in its pure pristine form but when it gets corrupted, it leads to corrupt decisions. There are examples based on Bedouin societies in North Africa where it can operate effectively. [343]

I have argued that drawing from the rich traditional of Islamic legal texts will also involve a critical interpretation of these texts. In addition, I have suggested that such crucial and progressive interpretation can be brought about through the harmonisation of Islamic law with the core values and ideals in international law discourse—such as justice, equality, and fairness. As I have demonstrated, there are deep affinities between Islamic law and international law. If the two are thought of in tandem and utilised accordingly, the conversation on change and progress in Afghanistan is likely to gain more acceptance, traction, and legitimacy.

Palestine/Israel

Moving now from Afghanistan, let us take up another case study through our critical, theoretical lens: the dispute between Palestine and Israel. This dispute frames geo-political discourse in the Middle East and is hugely important for international law and policy organisations. A peaceful resolution of this dispute has oft seemed challenging, but efforts to resolve it persist—and persist with fervour.

Let us begin by discussing some important recent events. In September 2020, the signing of the Abraham Accords by Israel, the United Arab Emirates (UAE), and Bahrain was hailed by the then US President Donald Trump as "marking the dawn" of a new Middle East.[344] By establishing diplomatic relations with Israel, the UAE and Bahrain overturned decades of non-recognition of Israel by the Arab Gulf states. Morocco and Sudan also followed suit, following which the US recognised Moroccan sovereignty over the Western Sahara and removed Sudan from its state sponsors of terrorism blacklist. Advocates of the Abraham Accords have pointed to the economic opportunities that may arise from tourism, trade, and the combination of Israeli technology with capital investments from the Gulf. However, since signing of the Accords, little in the region appears to have changed. While the strategic rationale of the Accords remains strong for the various parties, Israel's 11-day conflict with Hamas in May 2021 and ongoing tensions with the Palestinians serve as a reminder that the dynamics of the conflict are largely immune to external shifts.[345] The Middle East thus continues to be a region plagued by internal conflict.

Although the Biden administration has welcomed the Abraham Accords, negotiations with Iran over a return to the Joint Comprehensive Plan of Action (JCPOA) and the escalation in grey-zone conflict between Israel and Iran may have dampened the enthusiasm of other Arab Gulf states to draw closer to Tel Aviv. While Israel and the Arab Gulf states share concerns over Iran's regional activity and its nuclear weapons programme, they have yet to articulate a common approach to dealing with those threats.

One crucial aspect of the conflict between Palestine and Israel is the involvement of the US. Elgindy, questions the role that consecutive US administrations have played in attempting to broker a peaceful resolution to the Palestine–Israel conflict where the size and intensity of the blind spot have varied over the years from one administration to another. Elgindy exclaims:

> "Unless and until the US can over-come its blind spot to Israeli power and Palestine politics, its policies will be doomed to failure.[346]

Over the ensuing period, the conflict has come to the fore as a result of the Balfour Declaration in 1917 and the subsequent illegal usurpation of Palestinian land. These encroachments on Palestinian land were violations of international law in order to adhere to the Zionist ideology of creating a "Jewish Homeland." Coupled with this occupation is the principle of the "right to return" of Jews who have been subjected to anti-Semitism. This right is codified by law in Israel under the name 'law of return'. In 1950, Israel's Knesset passed a remarkable law, beginning with a few simple words that defined Israel's central purpose: "Every Jew has the right to immigrate to this country"[347] This was called the law of return and further cemented the status of Israel as a Jewish state.

It is important to stress here that within the rubric of Jewish tradition, not all ascribe to the Zionist viewpoint. Zionism is a political ideological movement that has utilised certain precepts of the Jewish faith tradition to justify, in their view, the principle of the right to return of Jews to their "Homeland" of Israel. However, these ideas and narratives continue to be dominant in the state of Israel—thus framing the dispute between Palestine and Israel on uniquely *religious* lines.

Intertwined in this conflict are the Arab citizens of Israel—called the Arab Israelis—who constitute more than one-fifth of Israel's total population.[348] They are citizens who proclaim to be the natural owners of the land in Israel that has been illegally taken away from them over a period of many decades via occupier settler movements, wars of aggression, and the revocation of fundamental human and economic rights. Despite having equal status and rights as citizens of Israel to their Jewish counterparts, the Arab Israelis face discrimination, and a lack of equality at a substantive level. They face discrimination that has shown to increase their poverty levels (the poverty rate of this community is thirty-six per cent, twice that of Jews in Israel); limited access to education and employment; and an acute lack of representation in politics and the public sphere.[349]

Now that we have an idea of the nature of the conflict between Israel and Palestine, and its religious undertones, we are well-equipped to discuss *how* Islamic law and international law can inform the debates on the Palestine–Israel conflict. The question I wish to pose in relation to this deep-rooted conflict in a land sacred to the three Abrahamic faiths is: how effective might the principles of international law and Islamic law be in helping to facilitate and broker a peaceful resolution to the conflict?

During my research for this book, I conducted interviews of certain strategic interlocuters who are exposed to the nuances of the conflict in the region and who have participated in conflict-resolution efforts. In particular, the interview with Jonathan Kuttab,[350] a non-violence conflict resolution attorney, highlights the nuances of the process of conflict resolution and the values that it must embody. Kuttab stressed that the framework for conflict resolution should be organised around principles of justice and human rights. He stated that there are fundamental problems with ideologies that are based on an absolutist model to conflict resolution and religion. For many, conflict resolution based on religion often rests an absolutist paradigm: if the divine has directed a particular way, principles of logic and self-interest become irrelevant as the attributes of God are "Absolute" in nature. For this reason, it is often believed that religion can end up undermining genuine conflict resolution.

Kuttab stressed that it is very important to differentiate the political movement of Zionism from the traditional normative tents of the religion of Judaism. There are many people and groups within the folds of the Jewish faith who do not support political Zionism. In light of the complex religious dynamic that frames the conflict, the resolution to the Palestine–Israel struggle requires a multi-lateral approach to bring about a just resolution. Kuttab is of the view that the resolution must come through the prism of a *one-state* framework that is based on democratic principles, the rule of law, and equality under the constitution. He therefore emphasises the importance of universal principles of equity and the rule of law—often the basis of public international law—as core principles in the resolution of conflict in the region.

As we have seen, the US has served as the chief sponsor and sole mediator in the peace process between Palestinians and Israelis. This has been both a blessing and a curse. On the one hand, as a superpower and Israel's closest ally in the region, the US is the only global actor sufficiently trusted by Israeli leaders to guarantee Israel's security. On the other hand, it also means that the peace process has been infused with idiosyncrasies of American politics, including Washington's sacred "special relationship" with Israel and the inordinate influence of the pro-Israel lobby. As Elgindy affirms:

> "This blindness to the unequal power dynamics between the Palestinians and Israel and the internal politics of both sides has critically hampered the ability of the U.S. to serve as an effective peace broker." [351]

With the emergence of an autonomous Palestinian national movement following Israel's conquest of the West Bank, East Jerusalem, and the Gaza Strip in 1967, American and Israeli officials were no longer able to ignore the political dimension of the Palestinian question. Although American and Israeli policymakers continue to marginalise the Palestinian Liberation Organisation (PLO), the umbrella organisation representing Palestinians worldwide, and to keep it out of the peace process, the issues that the Palestinian people face are now a matter of global interest and concern. With the Palestinian resistance movement gaining the traction and attention on a global stage, we see that a one-state solution focusing on the rights of Israelis is no longer a viable option. Instead, a two-state solution seems to be discussed by officials as the most viable way out of the conflict. Consider Tor Wennesland, Special Coordinator for the Middle East Peace Process at the UN, who stated in January 2022:

> Without a realistic prospect of an end to the occupation and the realisation of a two-State solution ... it is only a matter of time before we face an irreversible, dangerous collapse and widespread instability.[352]

We see, therefore, that, in the end, Washington's unique approach to peacekeeping has not succeeded. Indeed, by focusing on reassuring Israel and reforming the Palestinians rather than on changing the structural dynamics that sustained the conflict, most notably Israel's ongoing military occupation, the US-led peace process effectively reversed the standard model of mediation. They alleviated pressure on the stronger party and increased pressure on the weaker party.[353] This method is unsuccessful in effectively resolving conflict and ensuring that the rights of both parties are adequately secured.

In order to further understand the nuances at play here, we can undertake a brief overview of the methods and processes of dispute resolution in the region and the history of the conflict. The peace processes found inception, arguably, in the early 1990s. In 1994, Israel and the Palestine Liberation Organization (PLO) signed an Interim Agreement, which established the Palestinian National Authority (PA) and started a tortured "peace process." The implicit understanding was that this process would eventually lead to a two-state solution. The authority of the PA was to be gradually expanded and the territory under its control increased until it matured into a full-blown Palestinian state. The hard issues of Jerusalem, the refugees, final borders, security arrangements, and settlements were left to be eventually addressed as "final status issues."[354] Whether the parties had negotiated in good faith towards a genuine two-state solution, or whether the process was flawed from the start, the result was the same: settlements continued to expand and were solidified, this time with the apparent complicity and authorisation of the Palestinian leadership.

To show their commitment to peace and renunciation of "terrorism," the PA was required to stifle all forms of resistance by its own people and to forgo all forms of their national struggle, including nonviolent forms. They were also required to abate any calls for international intervention. When the Trump administration came into power, the right-wing settlers felt that they could get the US' approval to formalise their victories and force Palestinians into a total capitulation. Trump's "Deal of the Century" had their fingerprints all over it. The five difficult "final status" issues were all resolved in Israel's favour: Jerusalem was to be recognised as exclusively Jewish and under its sole sovereignty. There was to be no Palestinian right of return; and the status of refugees was to be solved by the Arab states, absolving Israel of any responsibility in that regard. No settlers were to be removed at all, and Israel would be free to annex settlement blocks as it chooses. Regarding Israeli security, it would retain supreme authority over all the land, including in the areas under "Palestinian control." External borders and border crossings would be permanently under Israel's control, and internal "borders" would be drawn and determined by Israel and the US.[355]

The interesting point here is that the language of two-state solution was not totally abandoned. Instead, it was specifically stated that statehood and sovereignty were "not exact terms, but their meaning could be determined by agreement of the parties."[356] In other words, if Palestinians would agree and act in complete accordance with the "Deal of the Century" (to Israel's satisfaction), they would be allowed to call themselves a state, and to call certain neighbourhoods outside the Wall "Jerusalem" or "Al Quds."

The fact that no Palestinians were found to accept this deal was immaterial. This was not to be a peace agreement between the two parties but rather a declaration of capitulation by Palestinians and a total victory by the Zionist movement. Its pronouncement marked the official death of any meaningful two-state solution.[357]

For anyone considering the claims of both Zionists and Palestinian Nationalists, the two-state solution presents a comfortable and convenient compromise to the dispute, as did the initial Partition Resolution of 1947. Perhaps the strongest reason for using two-state solution language is the fear of the alternative and the need to maintain a veto of one-state discussions.

To many Israeli liberals, as well as supporters of Israel worldwide, one state, if it is at all to be sustainable, will require a democratic "one person-one vote" component, which spells—in their minds—the end of the Jewish state and of Zionism. Meanwhile, Palestinians have consistently been told that to have any chance of peace, they need to abandon any thought of one state, and to work (against all odds) for a two-state solution. In this paradigm, the "demographic demon" makes it impossible to talk of *one-state*.[358]

These arguments make it difficult to abandon the two-state solution and explain why the language of two-state solution persists and dominates the conversation, even among those who acknowledge that it has no chance of ever becoming a reality. Once it is acknowledged that the two-state solution is no longer tenable and start seeking new solutions, it becomes necessary to consider what the two sides' minimum requirements are.

Those purists who insist on ignoring or denying the other party's legitimacy need not participate in this exercise. They will simply doom themselves and their people to eternal enmity and strife in a situation in which neither party can be fully successful.[359]

Responding to this, Kuttab proffers a solution whereby Minimum Requirements for Palestinians and Israelis are achievable, representing the best prospect for peace based on principles of citizenry and equality:

> "I personally have a vision for a new state that addresses the needs both of Israeli Jews and Palestinian Arabs. I believe this proposal addresses the needs of both communities, though achieving it may be an entirely different matter."[360]

Kuttab's vision is for a new entity, a state that is a hybrid, a unique entity in all the land of historic Palestine/Israel. This entity would embrace and validate the essential elements of both Zionism and Palestinian Nationalism, while rejecting those elements in each movement that degrade or deny the other. The vision will respect and recognise all three monotheistic religions and provide free access to people of all religions to their holy places in the Land. On Kuttab's construction, the new state will allow those who wish, as individuals or collective groups, to practice and order their lives in accordance with their religion. But it will also provide a secular system for personal status matters (marriage, divorce, inheritance) to those who do not wish to be bound by the religious structures of their group. The Constitution will guarantee several basic rights to all citizens, including the standard human rights to freedom of movement, speech, association, and freedom of religion. The Right of Return for anyone of Jewish or Palestinian ancestry will be guaranteed and will not be subject to parliamentary restriction by whoever is in the majority. The new state will continue to hold a special place for Jews worldwide and will continue to be important to all Jews who can look to it for cultural and religious focus, as well as a possible refuge in case of antisemitism and discrimination. At the same time, the new state will act as a centre of progressive life that can impact the Arab world. Palestinians can still be proud members of the Arab nation, while providing a progressive model for tolerant and enlightened life in the modern world.

It has been argued that no historical or current model exists where two or more diverse ethnic and religious communities have successfully created a peaceful and stable form of coexistence. The truth, however, is that there are several models where diverse communities have existed in peaceful cooperation. Kuttab does not refer simply to situations such as that in Lebanon, where a complex multi-ethnic constitution tried to balance different groups with difficulty, nor the failed Yugoslav tricameral system in which only a strong General Tito could keep Serbs, Muslims, and Croats at peace, and which dissolved into a system of warring entities on his death. Instead, he refers to pluralistic countries such as Canada, Belgium, Northern Ireland, and the modern US, where, with faltering steps, multi-ethnic societies have been established. Despite continuing tensions, racism, and discrimination by the majority, minorities have found legal protection and spaces to survive, thrive, and acquire identity as stakeholders in the national enterprise. [361]

But even if no successful model were to exist, the very uniqueness of the situation in the Holy Land, calls for a unique response and a new vision—a vision that would not only address the conflicting demands but that would also provide much, by way of example, to the surrounding countries and peoples. If we are to think of ways in which lasting peace and stability can be created in the region, we must take a bottom-up approach and ask how contextual practices can inform the process. I argue that by exploring the intersection of Islamic Law and international law, we can contribute meaningfully to the discussions on peacebuilding and conflict resolution in the region.

I shall establish this further based on the following *three lines of argument*. Cumulatively, it will become clear that in order to explain and frame the conflict in the Middle East, drawing from perspectives in Islamic law and international law is indeed crucial.

First, we must understand how Islamic law influences the legal system in Palestine. Islamic law is not a monolith and has a different cultural and social context depending on the region to which it is applied. Therefore, we must engage discursively and crucially with the *ways* in which Islamic law is unique in Palestine. While the legal system in Palestine is influenced by Islamic law, it still retains a resolutely pluralistic character. The law in Palestine—particularly the 'Basic Law'—clearly stipulates that Islam is central to the Palestinian legal system. Consider Article 4 below:

> Islam is the official religion in Palestine. Respect for the sanctity of all other divine religions shall be maintained. 2. The principles of Islamic Shari'a shall be a principal source of legislation. 3. Arabic shall be the official language.[362]

This demonstrates the significance of Shari'a on legislations in the region and the commitment of the Palestinian state to the principle of Islamic law. Even in areas relating to private law in Palestine, we see that the influence of Islamic law is immense. Scholars have emphasised that even though this focus on Islamic law is clear, there are several different interpretations of Islamic law that are prevalent—thus rooting Palestine in a model of 'legal pluralism'. Consider the work on the Palestinian legal system by Irene Schneider, who writes:

> The legal situation in Palestine generally and with regard to family law can be named as legally plural. Palestine has a rich legal history, today combining Ottoman, Jordanian, Egyptian, and Palestinian law, Israeli military law, and international law as applicable laws – as well as custom. Especially in the case of personal status law, the basis of the law are Islamic regulations that are constantly reconstructed and discussed and changed, as in the *khul'* ruling of 2012, thus reflecting the Islamic law in its different interpretations. Islamic law can thus be called "plural" in itself. Legal pluralism in the sense that the state or the legislature recognises the existence of a multiplicity of legal sources is thus confirmed for Palestine.[363]

Therefore, although rooted in principles of Islamic law, the legal system in Palestine can be characterised as embodying a distinctive form of legal pluralism.

Furthermore, we see that Islamic law in Palestine is framed through imminent international issues. The fact that Palestine has not been granted "statehood" in most international socio-political discourses has framed the region's tryst with Islamic law. In reviewing Robert H. Eisenman's book *Islamic law in Palestine and Israel*, Majid Khadduri summarises its main findings as follows:

> In other Arab countries, Islamic law has undergone considerable changes both in form and substance, but it was confirmed as territorial law. In the case of Palestine, the process has been reversed. Under British control, Islamic law was applied with virtually no changes in the domains in which it was not replaced by other laws, especially the Majalla (a code of civil law) and the law of personal status. After Israel was established, Islamic law was further restricted territorially by the introduction of Israeli legislation, but it preserved its personal character and remained binding on Muslims in all matters relating to personal status.[364]

Therefore, we see that Islamic law in Palestine is pluralistic and is restricted in its scope owing to Palestine's struggle for sovereignty. These factors frame the way in which international law is applied in the region and the forms it takes in shaping society and polity.

Second, and following on from this, it becomes important to re-imagine the Palestinian movement for liberation and identity *through* the core principles of Islamic law. Note that this is a substantive re-imagination—rather than a purely descriptive exercise that I have so far advocated for.

As I have mentioned in preceding discussions, the core idea behind Shari'a is to protect and promote five fundamental values: 1) life; 2) intellect; 3) reputation or dignity; 4) lineage or family; and 5) property. These are among the five objectives constituting Maqāṣid al-Shari'a, or part of the five core purposes and principles of Shari'a. Owing to the influence of these principles in Islamic law, and therefore on Palestine's legal system, we can better understand the main focus areas of the Palestinian fight for justice.

In one sense, the Palestinian people seem to be combining principles 1, 3, and 5—rather fundamentally, it must be said—in their struggle. At its essence, the Palestinian people are fighting for their right to land and life and livelihoods—which resonate with principles 1 and 5 outlined above. However, at an ideological level, this is also a fight for dignity and selfhood, that resonates with the third principle of Shari'a law. Cecil J. Hunt, in fact, frames the Palestinian fight as a struggle for *respect*. He suggests that:

> This perspective is vitally important because in this conflict, "respect is the number-one target ... and the first casualty."[365] This riddling of respect is

readily evidenced in the Israeli political rhetoric demeaning Palestinian humanity. For example, in a tone distressingly representative of the political mainstream of Israeli views of Palestinian humanity, there has been "a long [political] tradition of Israeli leaders implying that Palestinians are devoid of values, or not exactly human."[366]

Building on this analysis, which characterises respect as a central issue in the conflict, we see that Islamic law is and the principles of Shari'a also assert dignity or respect as a core human value. It is thus important to see the occupation of the Palestinian state as a matter of a denial of respect for the humanity of a people. Of course, several other issues such as land, violence, and livelihood also come into play here. The creation of an egalitarian state based on principles of equity, on the lines that Kuttab seems to imagine, may be one way to give Palestine the respect and dignity that its people rightly deserve.

Third, and finally, another way in which Islamic law and international law intersection at the ground level in this conflict is through the focus on dispute resolution and mediation that Palestinian leaders have sometimes encouraged. As I argued in Chapter 3, legal systems that are deeply informed by tenets of Islamic law are *more likely* to gravitate towards international settlement venues that resemble traditional Islamic law: these include third-party non-binding methods, such as conciliation and mediation. With this in mind, we see that the peace talks in the Middle East—which have been demanded by the Palestinians at several international fora—seem to have been the only remotely successful ways to establish peace.

The problem, however, is that the notions of peace under Islamic law refer to a *continuous and prolonged* sense of well-being, rather than fleeting diplomacy. This stability is lacking in the case of Palestine and Israel—wherein despite peace talks and agreements, unrest seems to resurface. In discussing the challenges faced in peacebuilding in the region, Rodolfo Ragionieri argues that the main question we need to consider is how to create sustainable peace in line with Islamic notions of peace:

> The question is, whether the peace process can bring a stable peace. Peace can be properly called "stable" (which is not always a synonym of "just") only if the actors involved have no interest in choosing any other feasible (or perceived as such) strategy.[367]

These three lines of argument show that paying closer attention to the intersection between Islamic law and international law in the conflict between Palestine and Israel is indeed timely and necessary. It is also crucial that Palestine is recognised as a state based on principles of sovereign equality which align with the concept of statehood in Islamic law.[368] The critical analysis provided here can help re-imagine the conflict and pave the way for discussions rooted in Islamic law that further peacebuilding efforts in the region.

Kashmir

The princely state of Kashmir has been a disputed territory between India and Pakistan since the time of the partition of the Indian subcontinent in 1947. It is a conflict that has led to three wars in the region between these neighbouring countries and has caused deep-rooted problems at a geo-political level in South Asia.

In 2018, the United Nations Human Rights Office of the High Commissioner published a *Report on the Situation of Human Rights in Kashmir: Developments in the Indian State of Jammu and Kashmir from June 2016 to April 2018, and General Human Rights Concerns in Azad Jammu and Kashmir and Gilgit-Baltistan.*[369] The report sets out the multiple human rights violations that have taken place in Indian-occupied Kashmir in particular and highlights the parties that have been complicit in these abuses. The Report emphasises the grievances of the Kashmiri people and calls for attention to be paid to their concerns.

On August 5, 2019, the Parliament in India voted in favour of a resolution to revoke the temporary special status granted under Art 370 of the Indian Constitution to Jammu and Kashmir.[370] The special or autonomous status granted to the state was a mechanism used by the people and movements in Kashmir to assert their identity and contend the violations of human rights that they often face at the hands of the Indian nation state and the Indian army. The Indian government also cut off communication lines in the valley, which were restored after five months. As part of the restrictive package, the Indian government also revoked Article 35-A, which was introduced through a Presidential order in 1954 to continue the old provision of the territory regulations under Article 370 of the Indian constitution.

These constitutional revocations and unjust restrictions led to regional and international condemnation of the actions of the Bharatiya Janata Party's (BJP) hard-line government, led by Prime Minister Narendra Modi. Many regional analysts have indicated that the moves orchestrated by India are an attempt to socially engineer the demographic and property rights of Indian-occupied Kashmir, changing it to that of a Hindu majority state at the expense of the Muslims who have been residing there for many years. Scholars have described the abrogation of Article 370 and the simultaneous restrictions put into effect in the region as a drastic human catastrophe—one that will have immense ramifications for the people of Kashmir and further the denial of their most fundamental human rights.[371]

As noted in previous chapters, based on classical Islamic law, the executive of a nation has the authority to declare "jihad" against whomever is deemed their enemy. A question that then arises is, what direction should be taken when dealing with "non-state actors" who carry out attacks against enemy groups and countries? India has continued to accuse Pakistan of using internationally proscribed groups such as Lashkar-e-Taiba (LET)[372] and Jaish-e-Mohammed (JM)[373] to undertake proxy attacks. Joel Hayward's view on such matters is that the concept of a "state" is a very modern concept, and it would be anachronistic to say that Prophet Muhammad created a state in his lifetime.[374] The Prophet created political organisations of sorts, but it had no geographical borders, no centralised government with assigned responsibilities, no codified body of law, no enforcement body (police force), and no fixed and countable population. According to Hayward, Jihad was not a political activity, but a religious activity and its initiation was for the cause of religious rather than political ambition.[375] After the Prophet's physical departure, warfare immediately changed from Jihad to organised political violence, but the title of *Jihad* was preserved as a means of creating acceptability for the activity of war among the faithful adherents.[376]

This resemblance does not create a religious legitimacy for groups such as Al Qaeda or Daesh to create a state in the modern Westphalian sense. Thus, the purpose of violence by these types of groups is disguised as a religious activity, i.e., Jihad, but its aim is something that the Prophet would neither have recognised nor endorsed.

When it comes to groups like the LET and JM, their objectives may not be intertwined with groups such as Daesh with regard to their aspiration to create a utopian so-called "Islamic state" as such. What they do seek to achieve, however, is to liberate the land of Kashmir from what they deem to be an illegal occupation. Such non-state groups also have the strategic aim of seeing Kashmir become part of Pakistan as opposed to India.

This is further complicated in terms of authenticity and legitimacy if the non-state actor groups' objectives are in exclusive alignment with that of a state. In this case, Pakistan would like to see an end of the illegal occupation of Kashmir by Indian troops. The state of Pakistan would also like to see the right of self-determination as enshrined in a UN Resolution being granted to the people of Kashmir to decide their own future. The non-state groups would most likely not wait for the process of self-determination to materialise and would most likely try to force the process. The modalities of the above have been covered by classical Islamic jurists. Hayward is of the view that a Jihad must be declared by an Emir, Caliph, or other recognised authority within the polity that has legitimacy bestowed on it by other polities around it.[377] An individual group on its own volition cannot self-declare and announce the calling to Jihad. So, if groups such as LET or JM are calling their followers to Jihad, whereas the Prime Minister of Pakistan, the President, or the Head of the Pakistan Army has not announced a state of jihad, then the *self-declared Jihad* of groups such as LET or JM would have no validity within the realm of Islamic law.

Considering the discussion and historical overview provided above, we can now proceed to examine what role international Islamic law and or diplomacy can play in helping to broker a peaceful resolution to this long-standing conflict and impasse in Kashmir. My aim—as with the previous sections on Afghanistan and Palestine and Israel—is to show how critical discourses from Islamic law that are harmonious with international law can play a crucial role in re-framing the discourses around the conflict in Kashmir.

With reference to international law, Pakistan and various other nations (excluding India) adopted United Nations Security Council Resolution (UNSCR) 39 on Kashmir in 1948. This resolution offered to assist in the peaceful resolution of the Kashmir conflict by setting up a commission of three members: one to be chosen by India, one to be chosen by Pakistan, and one to be chosen by the other two members of the commission. The commission was to write a joint letter advising the Security Council on what course of action would be best to help further peace in the region.[378] In 2020, the UN General Secretary Antonio Guterres called for the implementation of the UN Security Council Resolution on Kashmir, including the holding of a plebiscite among Kashmiri residents on whether they wanted to join India or Pakistan.

Since assuming office in 2018, the former Pakistani Prime Minister, Imran Khan (August 2018 to April 2022), has been championing the Kashmiri cause, including promising a plebiscite to Kashmiris as to whether they wished to be part of Pakistan or an independent nation. The Indian administration has not entertained the idea of an international broker playing a role to resolve the dispute and has constantly veered towards stating that it is a bilateral issue that needs to be resolved between the two countries without the intervention of a third party.

We see, therefore, that despite several efforts, Pakistan has laid out strict conditions to resume any form of dialogue with India, which includes India reinstating the revoked constitutional provisions of Articles 370 and 35A and a withdrawal of the Indian troops in Indian-occupied Kashmir. Kashmir itself was under a lengthy security lockdown and communication blackout between 2019 and 2021.[379]

Another key facet in the geo-political peace and reconciliation process between India and Pakistan is that both countries have nuclear capabilities. Some analysts would opine that by having such capabilities might have prevented the potential escalation of war between the neighbouring countries but there is always the caveat that nuclear weapons could make such scenarios more dangerous if they materialise.[380] Equally, there are proponents who would like to see a nuclear-free world, where the use of nuclear is used for energy as opposed to military purposes. The current dynamics and tensions between the two countries, however, make this an unrealistic hope.

Considering the pervasiveness of the conflict and the divisions along religious lines, I once again advocate for a rooted approach based in Islamic law and international law. I shall demonstrate this based on the following lines of argument.

First and foremost, Islamic law and theology have unequivocally stressed the importance of peace. Despite this, the Indian state and media routinely construct Islam and Islamic law as being "backward" or "regressive"—and are also prone to constructing Islam as a religion that endorses violence. The Modi hard-line BJP party that is misconstruing the normative teachings of the Hindu faith to stir anti-Muslim hatred based on the promulgation of the Hindutva ideology has not helped to facilitate peace between the two nuclear power states.

As Asma Afsaruddin notes, in an analysis of the discourse on peace in Islamic law and practice:

> Regardless of predominant discourses in the Western public sphere about Islam and Muslims today, it must be emphasised ... that the concept of peace is a central one in Islamic thought ... It is also well-known that Muslims traditionally greet one another by saying "Peace be on you" (As-sal ām ʿalaykum) to which the response is "And peace be on you" (Wa-ʿalaykum as-sal ām).[381]

We see that the goal of Islam is thus a just and peaceful social order. This is enshrined in the religious texts and is also interpreted as a core part of the practice of Islam. The characterisation that Islamic law and Muslims are not committed to the goal of peace is thus based not on truth or facts, but rather on propaganda.

Another relevant factor here is the pluralistic legal systems prevalent in India. India has a system of *personal laws*—wherein different personal laws, depending on religious communities, are applicable to members of different communities. The idea behind this was to allow for a model of secularism that enabled different religious identities and expressions to co-exist. The idea of India—as conceived of by its early leaders—was that of a secular nation-state that prides itself on the motto 'unity in diversity'.[382] However, with the advent of the pseudo[383]-Hindutva right wing ideology, we notice different perspectives being taken to the legal system as well. Most importantly, there has been a criticism and widespread devaluing of Islamic law and practices by the pseudo-Hindu nationalist government, led by Prime Minister Modi. Islamic law—or Muslim personal law as it is called in India—has been incorrectly characterised as being "backward" and unjust and steeped in discriminatory ideals, particularly on the lines of gender.

This propaganda has led to a famous dispute before the Indian Supreme Court on the legal status of *triple talaq*—a practice earlier protected by Muslim personal law. In the dispute of *Shayara Bano* v. *Union of India,* the court held that *tripple*—or *talaq-e biddat*—was unconstitutional. The court's ruling was based on whether this was an essential religious practice under Muslim law and seemed not to have paid adequate attention to the core issue in question, namely the issue of gender equality.[384] For our purposes here, the point is not whether *talaq-e-biddat* is in fact unjust in terms of gender equality. Rather, there is a need to emphasise that the way in which the Indian government constructs Islamic law is poignantly revealed through this dispute. Muslim personal law was further devalued in the Indian national and legal discourse.

Because of the prevalent anti-Islamic law attitude in India, there also is a demand—endorsed and even spearheaded by the present-day government in India—that seeks to establish a 'uniform civil code' in the country. This would serve to dismantle the system of personal law and disallow Indian Muslims from being governed by Islamic law even in the realm of family and private life. The uniform civil code and attempts to create it in India have been marked by scholars as an explicit "Hindu-ization" of the legal system in India, and a move to dismantle all other legal approaches—including Islamic law.

I argue not only that this propaganda against Islamic law is present internally in India but also that it is influencing and framing the dispute in Kashmir. The propaganda against Islamic law in India has led to the further targeting and victimisation of the Muslim minority in India. The Muslim Women (Protection of Rights on Marriage) Bill, 2019 was passed in the Indian Parliament. The bill makes the practice of instant triple talaq—which allows Muslim men to divorce their wives by uttering the word "talaq" thrice in spoken or written forms, or via electronic communication—a penal offence. Muslim men can be imprisoned for three years because of the legislation. Several civil society members have noticed that this legislation is blatantly anti-minority and paints Muslim personal law in a negative light. The lives of the Muslim minority have become worse off because the state can now easily target them, as a result of this legislation.

This propaganda against Islamic law and the systematic dismantling of Muslim personal law in India has affected the dispute in Kashmir. This propaganda against Islamic law contributes to the state-endorsed narrative that Islam is not a religion of peace and is instead rooted in notions of violence and terrorism. This has led to further repression of Kashmiris in the region; Kashmiris in Indian-occupied Kashmir are also influenced by these legal changes—wherein they can no longer choose to be governed by Muslim personal law. Anti-Muslim legislations may also be used to further target Kashmiris.

Therefore, the propaganda against Islamic law and the dismantling of the Muslim personal law system in India's domestic legal system has severe ramifications for the international law-governed dispute in Kashmir.

Acknowledging these issues—and indeed, tackling them through principles of peaceful dispute resolution —is essential and urgent need in Kashmir because the pseudo-Hindu nationalist government in India is also violating several human rights of Kashmiris. The violence that the people in Kashmir face, and the systemic issues that the occupation has brought, are oft discussed issues on the international stage.

However, we must also highlight—as I shall show now—that the occupation and oppression of Kashmiris targets certain core values or tenets in Islamic law. As I discussed in Chapter 3, one of the most important natural rights that citizens have under Islamic law and religious doctrine is the right to *dignity*. Human beings must be given dignity and respect—and this right is bestowed on human beings by the divine. Therefore, dignity holds a central place in Islamic law.

One core feature or extension of this idea of dignity is also the *dignity that must be given to the dead*. The management of dead bodies is a matter of dignity under Islamic law and is an issue of importance in the Qur'ān. As Ahmed Al-Dawoody writes:

> In Islam, human dignity is a right given by God to all humans—who are referred to in the Qur'ān as God's vicegerents on earth. Islam grants certain rights to humans before they are even born and others after their death. Whether dead or alive, the human body—created by God in the perfect shape—must be given dignity and respect. This importance of the human body is illustrated, for instance, in the Qur'ān 5:31.[385]

Now, it is a matter of most grave injustice that the victims of violence and atrocities in Kashmir are not given dignity even in death. In addition to the constant violation of individual dignity for Kashmiris during their lives, reports show that the rights of Kashmiris over dead bodies have not been respected. As Fahad Shah notes:

In the aftermath of August 2019 clampdown by New Delhi, when the BJP government revoked limited autonomy of Jammu and Kashmir and degraded it to a union territory, policy towards militancy was also changed. The government refused to hand over the bodies of the militants killed in combat and started burying them in discreet graveyards, far from Srinagar, in remote areas of north and central Kashmir. But as it happened: not only militants, but the government didn't return the bodies in alleged custodial killings[386] and extra-judicial gunfights.[387]

The government thus fails to protect not only the fundamental rights of Kashmiris, but also, importantly, certain fundamental rights that are held sacred under Islamic law and practice. This shows that the attack on Kashmiris is not an attack on Kashmiris merely as persons of the world. In fact, it is an attack on Kashmiris *as Muslims*—one that is targeted precisely against their religious identity.

This analysis shows the international community that the attack on Kashmiris is a result of their particular status as Muslims—and this is indicative of an anti-Muslim hatred attitude. I wish to note that it acts as a reminder of what Hannah Arendt—renowned political theorist and thinker—said about the attack against Jewish people during the Holocaust. Arendt theorises the attack against the Jewish community as a specific *religious attack*—it happened *because* of their status as Jews. She thus states that any retaliatory strategies must emphasise this very fact. Arendt writes:

"If one is attacked as a Jew, one must defend oneself as a Jew. Not as a German, not as a world-citizen, not as an upholder of the Rights of Man."[388]

Arendt's analysis is crucial to the Kashmiri question and is perhaps even of importance in the realms of Afghanistan and the Middle East, which I have discussed in this chapter. Arendt reminds us that religious conflicts must be attacked by drawing from *within* religious identities and discourses, rather than from outside them. When attacks against a people are associated with religion, response strategies must also refer to religion in order to counter-act an oppressive narrative.

I therefore suggest that considering the issues in all three of these areas—Afghanistan, Palestine and Kashmir—are conflicts against a people because of their identity as Muslims, any strategy to respond to these disputes must acknowledge this. What this entails is not that we must overtly adopt religious imaginations and defy the secular nature of international law and dispute resolution. Rather, it merely entails that we *draw from* Islamic law—clearly and imaginatively—to counteract the very discourses that perpetuate conflict and create division.

It is by bringing Islamic law perspectives into international law and practice on conflict resolution that we can pave the way towards the peaceful resolution of these disputes. This book has been an attempt to convey the importance of exploring international law through the lens of Islamic law. It has also attempted to show how, and why, such an analysis matters for the conflicts discussed in this chapter.

Towards a Theo-Diplomacy Paradigm

How can we bring Islamic law perspectives into international law for the peaceful resolution of disputes? How does one use international law, but embed it in the unique cultural context of Islamic law? Is there a distinctive *approach* or *paradigm* that we can rely on? Thus far, I have demonstrated how the intersection between Islamic and international law is valuable for each specific case study or theatre of conflict that I have identified. I shall now go on to sketch a general, overarching approach of *theo-diplomacy* and highlight the importance of such an approach for global conflict resolution and dispute settlement.

It is important to appreciate that in the realm of conflict resolution and peace and reconciliation, international statesman, diplomats, leaders, interlocutors, and politicians need to be well-versed in what I would term *theo-diplomacy*. I define theo-diplomacy as follows:

> Theo-Diplomacy is an approach wherein the interlocutors and advisers of the parties to a situation of conflict have religious literacy, appreciation and understanding of the contextual sensitivities of the conflict to help facilitate a pathway towards peace and reconciliation.

Drawing on this rough idea, we can specify some more contours to this approach. First, *theo-diplomacy* provides a faith-based conflict resolution and diplomatic approach that very much aligns with the tenets of the Islamic framework to conflict resolution, arbitration and peacebuilding. It provides a model which espouses civic, political, and religious authority, and counsel and representation based on mutual respect of other faith traditions within the rubric and spirit of the Hudaybah model (629 CE), where, as part of the process of truce, other parties and groups could also enter into the peaceful agreement.

Second, this model of *theo-diplomacy* that I have outlined aligns with contemporary approaches in the scholarship but indeed develops the core ideas further and extends them to conflict resolution and peacebuilding in the context of international law. For instance, the *theo-diplomacy* approach ties in well with the findings of the *Islamic Relief Guide* on an Islamic framework of peacebuilding that collates extensive research on faith-based development in an international context. According to the analysis conducted in this report:

> Islamic peacebuilding frameworks and methods aim to restore or rebuild a natural tendency among humans to be in sync with their Creator. It assumes that people can change through reason and compassion.[389]

The approach of *theo-diplomacy* also finds affinity with other contemporary approaches to peacebuilding. In his book *Nonviolence and Peace Building in Islam: Theory and Practice,* Mohammed Abu-Nimer presents a framework on peacebuilding that is informed by Islam. He builds his account on the following three principles: justice, social empowerment, and unity.[390]

This connects well with our discussion so far. As I have discussed, intertwined in the international conflict resolution framework is the important topic of Islamic peacebuilding approaches where faith-based development and organisations can play a pivotal role in international relations from a humanitarian perspective. In the *Islamic Relief Practitioners' Guide*, we further see an emphasis on the Islamic understanding of peacebuilding as a central aspect of any framework:

> "The Islamic understanding of peace can be defined as a process through which human beings can establish foundations for interacting with each other and with nature in harmony, instituting just social-economic structures where human beings can flourish and fulfil their potential." [391]

The *theo-diplomacy* approach shows, in particular, that a situation of balance and equilibrium is critical for Islam's approach to peacebuilding. A simplistic description of peace as an absence of violence involves a differentiation between "negative peace" as being a superficial state of peace and "positive peace" as something providing more assurance to individuals without fear or reprimand for their economic, social, and physical security. There is also the view that such descriptions of peacebuilding are merely idealised aspirational statements and do not correspond to the realities on the ground. The juxtaposition to this view is that without strategic understanding, dispute resolution, and legal and international frameworks in peacebuilding, it is difficult to bring the opposing parties to a consensus.

The core values and principles that inform an Islamic understanding of peace and non-violence are crucial in the theo-diplomatic model to bring about peace and reconciliation in practice. The *Islamic Relief Practitioner Guide* focuses lists these core values as:

- Universality, dignity and sacredness of humanity through the principle of the original nature of human beings (fitrah)
- Social empowerment by doing good (khayr and ihsan) through the principle of stewardship (khilafah).
- Pursuit of justice, equality and fairness through the principle of justice (adl).
- Transformation of relationships and rehumanisation through the principles of compassion and mercy (rahman and rahim).
- Reconciliation and healing through the principles of pardoning and forgiveness (afu and musamaha).
- Nonviolent and creative solutions to problems through the principle of patience (sabr).
- Quest for peace through love (hubb) and the principle of loving-kindness (mawadda).[392]

One can see how the principles of operation of faith-based organisations such as Islamic Relief very much align with the tenets of international and Islamic law that have been discussed in this book. The effectiveness of such organisations in the charitable, humanitarian space plays a meaningful role in brokering resolutions to conflicts and tend to come into play in the post-intervention or post-conflict stage rather than in the pre-conflict stage. The plights of innocents in conflict, and their humanitarian needs, as highlighted by organisations such as Human Rights Watch, Amnesty International, and the United Nations on the international stage, can certainly heighten the need for a de-escalation of tensions in conflict hot spots around the world. Recent reports on the situation in Palestine,[393] Afghanistan[394] and previously in Kashmir,[395] as well as the plight of the Uyghurs in China[396] are examples of this. The immediacy of a readily credible resolution of such efforts is difficult to gauge, but what such organisations and the raising of the plight of victims of atrocity crimes, injustice, and oppression do is to bring their plight to the attention of the global media. This can trigger the opening of certain diplomatic dialogue tracts, but it can also potentially antagonise parties to a conflict further who feel that the way the reports have been compiled are biased and not an accurate depiction of the realities of the ground.[397]

The theo-diplomacy paradigm that I propound can also be explored from the perspective of third-party mediators in conflict resolution and peacebuilding processes. These mediators need to have a pulse on the social, cultural, and religious contextual norms of the groups involved in a conflict and must also be impartial and able to listen well. Faith actors are viewed as authoritative representatives that can have a pivotal role in this regard, along with women who can be advocates for women's rights while respecting cultural and religious sensitivities. It is imperative if peace is to have a long-lasting legacy that a broad representation from a cross-section of the religious, social, economic, and cultural divide have a stake in negotiations in order for the process of healing and reconciliation take place.

The theo-diplomacy model or paradigm has evolved through our understanding of specific conflicts such as those in Afghanistan, Palestine and Israel, and Kashmir. From the particularities of these contexts, we arrive at a general theoretical understanding or model of *how* the interaction between international and Islamic law can be reconciled meaningfully through the *theo-diplomacy approach*. This understanding must transcend the realpolitik tit for tat that politicians, diplomats, and interlocutors often get engrossed in for it to be effective. It is through such a middle-ground between Islamic law and international law—and indeed between the particular and the universal—that we can find a way to reframe and resolve international disputes in a peaceful manner.

References

Abu-Nimer, Mohammed. *Nonviolence and Peace Building in Islam: Theory and Practice*. Gainesville: University Press of Florida, 2003.

Ahmed Al-Dawoody, *Respect for the Dead under Islamic Law: Considerations for Humanitarian Forensics,* Humanitarian Law and Policy, https://blogs.icrc.org/law-and-policy/2018/11/01/respect-for-the-dead-under-islamic-law-considerations-for-humanitarian-forensics/ (Accessed 18th December 2022).

Ahlawat, Dalbir, and M. Raymond Izarali. "India's revocation of Article 370: Security dilemmas and options for Pakistan." *The Round Table* 109, no. 6 (2020): 663–683.

Afsaruddin, Asma. "The Concept of Peace in Islam". *The Concept of Peace in Judaism, Christianity and Islam*, edited by Georges Tamer, Berlin, Boston: De Gruyter, 2020, pp. 99-158.
https://doi.org/10.1515/9783110682021-003

Akbar Ahmed, Remembering the Wali of Swat (dailytimes.com.pk) June 24, 2020

Arendt, Hannah, Jerome Kohn, Essays in Understanding, 1930-1954: Harcourt, Brace & Co, New York, 1994.

Anastasiya Hozyainova, USIP Special Report 347, *Sharia and Women's Rights in Afghanistan."* March 2014, 1-10.
SR347-Sharia_and_Women's_Rights_in_Afghanistan.pdf (usip.org) (Accessed January 2, 2022)

Dr. *Azeem Ibrahim et al, The Uyghur Genocide: An Examination of China's Breaches of the 1948 Genocide Convention - New Lines Institute* (Accessed 18th December 2021).

BBC News, "Yemen crisis: Why is there a war?" (2 November 2021), https://www.bbc.com/news/world-middle-east-29319423

Beckett, Tom, Ambassador Nancy Jamal, Dr Yoel Guzansky, Dr Hasan Alhasan, "The Abraham Accords: Evolving Partnerships, Persistent Challenges," September 27, 2021. The Abraham Accords: Evolving Partnerships, Persistent Challenges (iiss.org) (Accessed December 16th, 2021).

Cecil J. Hunt II., A Poverty of Respect: Human Rights, Honor, Dignity and Respect in the Israeli-Palestinian Conflict, 71 ALB. L. REV. 2008, 862-3.

Caitlin Talmadge, *Are nuclear weapons keeping the India-Pakistan crisis from escalating—or making it more dangerous? (brookings.edu),* March 8, 2019. (Accessed 18th December 2022).

Pakistan countering 'West-backed' Indian military build-up: National Command Authority aide - Pakistan - DAWN.COM (Accessed 30th June, 2022)

Durrani, A. "Strategic Decision Making in Pakistan." *Institute of Strategic Studies Islamabad* (1 September 2013): 1–22, https://issi.org.pk/strategic-decision-making-in-pakistan/ (Accessed December 6, 2021).

Pakistan is losing patience with the Taliban | The Economist (Accessed 30th June, 2022)

Elgindy, K. *Black Spot. American and the Palestinians, from Balfour to Trump*. Washington, DC: Brookings Institution Press, 2019.

Elgindy, Khaled. *Blind Spot: America and the Palestinians, from Balfour to Trump*. Brookings Institution Press, 2019.

Emon, Anver M. *Religious Minorities and Islamic Law: Accommodation and the Limits of Tolerance*. Oxford: Oxford University Press.

UK withdrawal from Afghanistan was a 'disaster' and 'betrayal' | Financial Times (ft.com) (Accessed 30th June 2022)

Fahad Shah, *Graveyard on a hill: Where do Kashmir's dead go?*, The Kashmir Walla, November 2021, https://thekashmirwalla.com/graveyard-on-a-hill-where-do-kashmirs-dead-go/ (Accessed 18th December 2022).

Fundamental Principles of the Democratic Republic of Afghanistan, April, 20, 21 (1980) (SAUR 1, 1359, AH), 6-7. Fundamental Principles of the Democratic Republic of Afghanistan: Publication Department, Ministry of Information and Culture, Government Printing House: Free Download, Borrow, and Streaming : Internet Archive (Accessed 30th June, 2022).

George Wright, *BBC India offices searched by income tax officials - BBC News* (Accessed March 17, 2023).

Gottlob, Michael. "India's unity in diversity as a question of historical perspective." *Economic and Political Weekly* (2007): 779–789.

Hamid Khan, Opinion Contributor, *Taliban doesn't equal Islam: How News Coverage of Afghanistan Disserves a Great Religion*, USA Today Opinion, August 21, 2021. Taliban and Islam: Why extremism doesn't reflect a great religion (usatoday.com) (accessed January 2, 2022).

Hayward, J. *The Leadership of Muhammad: A Historical Reconstruction*. Brynmill: Claritas Books, 2021.

Author Interview with Hayward, J, September 22nd, 2021.

Herklotz, Tanja. "Shayara Bano versus Union of India and Others. The Indian Supreme Court's Ban of Triple Talaq and the Debate around Muslim

Personal Law and Gender Justice," *Verfassung und Recht in Übersee/Law and Politics in Africa, Asia and Latin America* 50, no. 3 (2017): 300–311.

Islamic Republic of Afghanistan, The Constitution of Afghanistan, (Ratified) January 26, 2004. Microsoft Word - The Constitution of the Islamic Republic of Afghanistan (afghanembassy.com.pl) (Accessed 30th June, 2022).

UK Government recognition of the State of Palestine alongside the State of Israel - House of Commons Library (parliament.uk), 21 February 2022 (Accessed 30th June 2022).

Hunt II., Cecil J. *A Poverty of Respect: Human Rights, Honor, Dignity and Respect in the Israeli-Palestinian Conflict*, 71 ALB. L. REV. 861 (2008).

Interview: For Palestinians in Gaza, Freedom is Priceless | Human Rights Watch (hrw.org) (Accessed 30th June 2022)

Conflict in Afghanistan: A new regional security map and state-building implications since the Taliban takeover (iiss.org) (Accessed 30th June 2022)

Kadayifci-Orellana, S. Ayse, Mohammed Abu-Nimer, and Amjad Mohamed-Saleem. "Understanding an Islamic Framework for Peacebuilding," *Islamic Relief Worldwide, Working Paper Series No* (2013).

Khadduri, Majid. Book review of Eisenman, Robert H. *Islamic Law in Palestine and Israel: A History of the Survival of Tanzimat and Sharī'a in the British Mandate and the Jewish State.* Vol. 26. Brill, 1978, *Middle East Journal* 33, no. 3 (1979).

Khan, H. M. "Islamic Law, Customary Law, and Afghan Informal Justice." *United States Institute of Peace*, https://www.usip.org/publications/2015/03/islamic-law-customary-law-and-afghan-informal-justice (Accessed 16th December 2021)

Khan, Robina, Muhammad Zubair Khan, and Zafar Abbas. "Moving towards human catastrophe: the abrogation of Article 370 in Kashmir Valley." *Journal of Muslim Minority Affairs* 41, no. 1 (2021): 78–85.

Kuttab, Jonathan. *Beyond the Two State Solution.* Washington, DC: Nonviolence International, 2021.

Mir-Hosseini, Ziba. "Muslim Women's Quest for Equality: Between Islamic Law and Feminism." *Critical Inquiry* 32, no. 4 (Summer 2006): 629–645

Dr. R. McCallum, *Muslims, Christians and Peace, United Nations Peacekeeping,* CMCS, Oxford, 2022. Muslims, Christians and Peace — Centre for Muslim-Christian Studies (cmcsoxford.org.uk) (Accessed 30th June 2022)

Mohammad Hashim Kamali, *Against extremism: the middle path of moderation*, Foundazione Oasis, September 13, 2021. https://www.oasiscenter.eu/en/against-extremism-the-middle-path-of-moderation (Accessed January 2, 2022).

Nadjma Yassari, Mohammad Hamid Saboory, *Sharia and National Law in Afghanistan, 2010.*
https://www.juragentium.org/topics/islam/en/yassari.htm (Accessed 30 June, 2022).

Office of the United Nations High Commissioner for Human Rights, *Report on the Situation of Human Rights in Kashmir: Developments in the Indian State of Jammu and Kashmir from June 2016 to April 2018, and General Human Rights Concerns in Azad Jammu and Kashmir and Gilgit-Baltistan* (14 June 2018),
https://www.ohchr.org/Documents/Countries/PK/DevelopmentsInKashmirJune2016ToApril2018.pdf. (Accessed 17th December 2021).

PBS, "A Historical Timeline of Afghanistan." August 30, 2021, https://www.pbs.org/newshour/politics/asia-jan-june11-timeline-afghanistan. (Accessed 17th December 2021).

Ragionieri, Rodolfo. "The peace process in the Middle East: Israelis and Palestinians." *International Journal of Peace Studies* 2, no. 2 (1997): 49–65,

Rhodes, B. "Inside the White House During the Syrian 'Red Line' Crisis." *The Atlantic*, June 3, 2018), Available online at:
https://www.theatlantic.com/international/archive/2018/06/inside-the-white-house-during-the-syrian-red-line-crisis/561887/ (accessed 18th December 2021).

Robina Khan, Muhammad Zubair Khan & Zafar Abbas, *Moving Towards Human Catastrophe: The Abrogation of Article 30 in Kashmir Valley*. Journal of Muslim Minority Affairs, 41:1, 78-85.

Robina Khan, Muhammad Zubair Khan & Zafar Abbas, *Human Catastrophe: The Abrogation of Article 370 in Kashmir Valley*, Journal of Muslim Minority Affairs, 41:1, 78-85,

Richard Ben Cramer, *How Israel Lost: The Four Questions,* Simon & Schuster, *London, 2004.*

Schiwal, Julia. "Two Futures for Religious Minorities in Afghanistan," LSE Blogs, https://blogs.lse.ac.uk/religionglobalsociety/2021/08/two-futures-for-religious-minorities-in-afghanistan/ (Accessed December 18th 2021).

Schneider, Irene, and Nijmi Edres, eds. *Uses of the Past: Sharī'a and Gender in Legal Theory and Practice in Palestine and Israel.* Lara-Lauren Goudarzi-Gereke, *Perspectives on Palestinian Family Law*, 1st ed. Harrassowitz Verlag, 2018, 47-68. https://doi.org/10.2307/j.ctvcm4fxc/ https://doi.org/10.2307/j.ctvcm4fxc.6. (Accessed December 18th, 2021)

Security Council Resolution 2139 (2014) (22 February 2014) UN Doc S/RES/2139 (2014). Available online at: https://www.securitycouncilreport.org/atf/cf/%7B65BFCF9B-6D27-4E9C-8CD3-CF6E4FF96FF9%7D/s_res_2139.pdf (accessed December 18th, 2021)

Singh, Mahendra Pal, and Surya Deva. "The constitution of India: Symbol of unity in diversity." *Jahrbuch des Offentlichen Rechts der Gegenwart, Yearbook of Public Law (Germany)* 53 (2005): 649–686.

Sohail. H. Hashmi, "Islamic Political Ethics: Civil Society, Pluralism, and Conflict, Princeton University Press, 2002.

Tim Foxley and Dr. Antonio Giustozzi, *A Force of Moderation or Radicalisation? The Role of Afghanistan's Ulema | Royal United Services Institute (rusi.org)*, 26 January 2023. (Accessed February 18, 2023).

Yashraj Sharma, "India is forcing us to pick guns": Kashmir mourns death of 26-yr-old in custody (thekashmirwalla.com), 16 September, 2020. (Accessed 18th December 2022).

CHAPTER FIVE

CONCLUSION

Abstract

In this concluding chapter, a final assessment will be made of which of the conflict resolution, arbitration, and peace and reconciliation methodologies—if any—are the best models to use in the conflict theatres across the world. The concept of "theo-diplomacy," which I have laid out in the preceding chapter, will inform the discussions in this chapter. My goal is to examine what faith-based conflict resolution and diplomacy entails in a theo-diplomacy based framework. The chapter will also examine what makes a conflict resolution effort fall within the rubric of "theo-diplomacy"—and how faith-based approaches, rooted in universal principles, can be forged at the intersection of international and Islamic law. This chapter also opens new questions that I hope will be examined in future research in these areas.

In this book, I have assessed the various tools that are available for international arbitrators, interlocutors, adjudicators, nation states, and supranational organisations when undertaking conflict resolution, arbitration, and peace and reconciliation initiatives. The remit of this book has been to focus on selected conflict theatres—Palestine–Israel, Afghanistan, and Kashmir—that have been centre stage in recent history. My objective was to explore the rich heritage, legacy, tools, principles, and methodologies of Islamic law on the themes of conflict resolution, peace, and reconciliation in these selected conflict theatres in order to help broker a peaceful resolution to these conflicts.

While it is difficult to draw definite conclusions as to whether the introduction, use, and application of Islamic Law would help to accelerate or facilitate the brokering of a peaceful resolution to these conflicts, we can certainly say, after the analysis outlined in the book, that the principles and ethics of Islamic law provide an excellent framework *if interpreted and applied correctly*. This is made clear in the context of the conflict theatres in which Islamic norms are part and parcel of the rubric of those states.

For instance, for countries such as Afghanistan, the judicial interpretation, and models of the schools of Islamic law may differ based on the spirit and application of the holistic aspects of Islamic law. As I have shown in Chapter 4, then, what is crucial is the *interpretation* of Islamic law in a manner that is informed by principles in Islamic law. The direction of travel should be orientated towards equilibrium, moderation, justice, and mercy based on the true essential tenets of the Islamic tradition, as opposed to pseudo-reformist misinterpretations and understandings that can end up stifling the pathway towards peace and reconciliation as opposed to facilitating it. Critical and progressive interpretations of Islamic law, as I have discussed in Chapter 4, are therefore the need of the hour.

In conflict theatres such as Palestine–Israel and, for that matter, Kashmir, the exclusive focus on Islamic law as the main source and tool for conflict resolution can potentially hinder, rather than facilitate peace-building and Islamic law must be supplemented with strong protections for minorities. For countries in which Islamic legal ethics and norms are not the main foundation of those societies, suffice it to state that alternative rules-based structures would need to be observed and implemented for those states to function in a harmonious manner. Let us take the situation of the disputed territory of Kashmir or the Palestine–Israeli conflict, for instance: attempting to introduce a purely religious-based Islamic law conflict resolution absolutist model could end up hindering the process towards peace and reconciliation as the parties involved will not feel obliged to be bound by the absolutist dictates that are derived from Islamic law.

At this juncture, it is important to stress that while for many in contemporary society the principles of Islamic law or religious tenets may be viewed as absolutist in their dimension, a true understanding and appreciation of Islamic law that hopefully this book has elucidated will demonstrate that the tools and principles of Islamic law are in fact diverse and flexible. Islamic law is not a vertical ruling mechanism and methodology, but one that is very much holistic in its nature and spirit.

An important area for additional research is the immense synergy that exists between the principles of Islamic law, international law, and international humanitarian law. On the themes of human rights, self-defence, pre-emptive strikes, the protection of civilians, the status of women, places of worship, religious leaders, atrocities, crimes against humanity, terrorism, torture, and genocide, as well as upholding the principles of justice, fairness, and humanity one will find many junctures at which there is universal alignment with certain variations on specific elements between the different realms.

Conclusion

The observation and analysis that I have been able to undertake on the global theatres of conflict such Afghanistan, Palestine–Israel and Kashmir lead one to the conclusion that by focusing on the synergies that exist in the lofty principles of international law, international humanitarian law, and Islamic law, one may provide a greater opportunity and hope for the parties to the dispute to reach a stage of common agreement, resolution, and peace and reconciliation. The standardisation and universalisation of the principles of justice, human rights, and accountability hold greater weight and leverage in the global polity and realm of international dispute resolution than the specificities of a particular religious ideology. This supposition does not in any way delineate or abrogate the importance of religious principles, ethics and norms but rather looks to amalgamate those very principles to universally accepted ideals and principles across the international comity of nation states and humanity at large. It is also important to synergise the ethics and principles of Islamic law and International Law to the local dimension, context and variation of conflict theatre based on the principle of subsidiarity for there to be a meaningful likelihood towards peace and reconciliation.

As part of this conclusion, it would be befitting for me to cite two leading authorities in the realm of Islamic and international humanitarian law on the modalities of conflict resolution, peace, and reconciliation. Both conclude, in their unique ways, that the sanctity and protection of human life is of paramount importance. Professor Joel Hayward, who focuses on the Qur'an, reaches the conclusion that the Qur'an is unambiguous: Muslims are prohibited from undertaking offensive violence and are always compelled, if defensive warfare should become unavoidable, to act within a code of ethical behaviour.[398] This is closely akin to, and compatible with the Western warrior code embedded within the Just War doctrine.

Furthermore, Dr Ahmed Al-Dawoody lays down the key foundation stones and principles of Islamic Humanitarian law in the following passage on the interpretation and application of Islamic regulations:

> ... the attention of the classical Muslim jurists was primarily directed towards two considerations: firstly, not to endanger the lives of non-combatants; and secondly, not to destroy enemy property except as a military necessity or as a reprisal. These concerns are of course on top of the primary goal of winning the war. The importance of the sanctity and humanity of the human soul in the Islamic tradition is illustrated in the rules that prohibit attacking non-combatants, using weapons that do not discriminate between combatants and non-combatants, attacking human shields, or attacking the enemy at night. In addition, the humane treatment of prisoners, as ordered by the Prophet Muhammad and mentioned in the Qur'an, underlines the requirement to preserve human dignity in wartime, a

concept which is also illustrated by the rules against attacking an enemy in the face or mutilating their body after death. Respect for the enemy also includes the requirement not to destroy enemy property during hostilities except in cases of military necessity, a principle which is also demonstrated by jurists' deliberations over the permissibility of Muslims' animals to eat the fodder of the enemy.[399]

Dawoody is of the view that many violations of international law would no longer occur if people lived by the words of Imām 'Alı ibn Abı Țālib, who said: "There are two types of people: your brothers in religion or your peers in humanity."[400]

A very important point that needs to be appreciated at this juncture is that while the remit of this book has focused on the principles of Islamic law in specific theatres of conflict, there is a diverse range of faith traditions prevalent in these regions. Take the case of Palestine–Israel, where we have representation from the major Abrahamic faith traditions of Judaism, Christianity, and Islam. In the case of Palestine–Israel, any conflict resolution would entail having a consortium of senior counsel of advisers (Clergy, Imams, Rabbis, Priests, etc.) who are well versed in the theological traditions and could help to steer the negotiations between the disputed parties to universally accepted principles of peace and reconciliation. In the case of Kashmir, where there is a prominent representation from the Islamic, Sikh, Hindu, and Christian traditions, the principles of dispute resolution would also thus be informed by this religious plurality.

The raison d'etre as to why *theo-diplomacy* has a greater likelihood of success in the selected conflicts that I have covered in this book is that it provides the theological authoritative framework, along with the contextual, cultural, diplomatic, and political understanding of the sensitivities that exist between disputing parties to drive towards a peaceful resolution. An example where *theo-diplomacy* has been successful seems to be in the "A Common Word Between Us and You" (ACW) initiative that was launched on 13 October 2007. This initially took the form of an open letter signed by 138 leading Muslim scholars and intellectuals to the leaders of the Christian churches and denominations of the entire world, including his Holiness Pope Benedict XVI. The proposal was based on verses from the Holy Qur'an and Holy Bible, that Islam and Christianity share, at their cores, the twin "golden" commandments of the paramount importance of loving God and loving one's neighbour. Based on this common ground, it called for peace and harmony between Christians and Muslims worldwide; it also extended the global handshake of interreligious goodwill, friendship, and fellowship and, consequently, of world peace.[401] While opening the hands of friendship and cooperation in the ACW was between Islam and

Christianity, the principle and essence of the message very much resonates for all faith traditions and indeed humanity at large. A more recent Islamic orientated attempt along similar lines organised by the Muslim World League (MWL) is the Makkah Declaration in 2019 which was signed by 1,200 figures from the Muslim world following a landmark gathering in the holy city of Makkah. The Declaration stated that religious and cultural diversity did not justify conflict and that civilised dialogue was the pathway to overcoming historical difference.[402]

From such illustrations, we see that *theo-diplomacy*—as I have articulated it in the course of this book—can be a promising new approach to conflict resolution. A pertinent question to ask at this juncture is what makes a conflict fall within the purview of *theo-diplomacy*. My aim is not to strictly specify the approach's contours, but rather to lay down the idea behind the approach and demonstrate its distinctiveness. Still, a starting point would be to infer whether the individual or organisations involved hold religious authority in a particular region. If one applies this to the Palestine–Israeli conflict, it is not always the case that the parties with whom one must negotiate to broker a peaceful resolution will have the authority or backing of their respective countries and base. If the political parties in Palestine and Israel have been elected democratically, that would be sufficient even in a framework of Islamic law for them to have the assumed authority to warrant being consulted. Similarly, in the case of Afghanistan, the Taliban's modus operandi is heavily based on religious and ideological doctrine in its political and leadership strata, but such ideology would not necessarily be recognised as authoritative by many co-religionists in the country and internationally. But, once again, what makes the conflict in Afghanistan fall within the purview of *theo-diplomacy* is the strong sway towards the religious components particularly Islam that play a pivotal role in the governance, administration, and conflict resolution processes of the country.

What is often overlooked by observers and political analyst of Afghanistan is the diverse religious heritage of the country. For instance, Sh. Hamza Yusuf in his essay "Buddha in the Qur'an?" cites:

> Buddhism thrived during the early period of the Muslim conquests, and historical accounts describe in great detail the temples and Buddhist schools in places such as Balkh and Mazaar-e-Sharif in today's northern Afghanistan … The keepers of one of the most important shrines in Buddhist history were Persian-speaking Afghans, known as the Barmakids, who were brilliant Buddhist administrators. After their conversion to Islam, they were brought to Baghdad during the rule of the Abbasid dynasty, where they revolutionised Muslim government and introduced important diplomatic innovations that changed the face of Islam.[403]

What the above passages demonstrates is the deep-rooted religious heritage and history that groups like the Taliban have oft neglected in their religious depiction and practical application and interpretation of Islamic law. These neglected key components of theological history, ethics, and what in Islamic law is termed "urf," must be accommodated within the contextual theo-diplomatic model that I have proposed.

If one looks to apply the *theo-diplomacy* conflict resolution model to the situation in Kashmir, some interesting paradigms can be drawn out. The democratically elected leadership of the countries neighbouring the conflict zone all ascribe to religious teachings and models. As I discussed earlier, the religious- ideological narrative which underpinned Pakistan's Imran Khan-led government has been at odds with the religious-ideological narrative of India's Narendra Modi-led government. Furthermore, the parties involved in the long-standing Kashmir conflict are not just those from the leadership echelons of India and Pakistan (e.g., foreign ministers and diplomatic aids), but also separatist, pro-Pakistan, and pro-India leaders and parties.[404] A. Hashim and R. Fareed argue that groups such as the Jammu and Kashmir Liberation Front (JKLF), Hizb-ul-Mu-jahideen (HUM), the Jaish-e-Muhammad (JEM), and the Lashkar-e-Taiba (LeT) also play a crucial role in the conflict in Kashmir.[405]

Applying the *theo-diplomacy* model of conflict resolution in Kashmir, where there is a plurality of groups and political parties with religious, secular, political, and ideological motivations for their involvement in the conflict, draws out some interesting paradigms. From an Islamic Law perspective, while the democratically elected leaders of the respective nation states have the political authority to attempt to broker a peaceful outcome, the groups and organisations—despite being driven by a religious motivation in their membership—may not always adhere to the core principles and tenets of Islamic law when it comes to the mechanisms and means adopted to resolve the conflict.

The Kashmir conflict is thus ultimately about ownership of land, as well as ensuring fully fledged civil, economic, and political rights for citizens to live freely without discrimination. It is also about their right to choose in a democratic manner whether they would like to be an independent state, or part of Pakistan or India. Based on 2011 census data for Jammu and Kashmir, 68.3 per cent of the population were Muslim, 28.4 per cent were Hindu, 1.9 per cent Sikh, 0.9 per cent Buddhist, and 0.3 per cent Christian.[406] It is the religious component of the population of the disputed territory that brings the *theo-diplomacy* model of conflict resolution into play.

It is here where I advocate that a senior council of authoritative religious advisers from the faith traditions that are represented in Kashmir can provide guidance to the diplomats and interlocutors who are working to broker a peaceful resolution to the conflict. By having a body of senior authoritative religious advisers who are well-versed in their traditions and who have an appreciation of the different scriptural sources across the faith traditions with regard to principles of peace, and racial and religious harmony increases the likelihood of being able to facilitate a peaceful outcome to the conflict.

There does not appear to be previous examples of the *theo-diplomacy* model that I am advocating being used in practice to broker a resolution to the Kashmir conflict. By using the theo-diplomatic model, we may reduce the likelihood of violent extremist interpretations and organisations bringing their extreme views and practices to the fore to misrepresent the core tenets of the faiths that they claim to represent. Such a *theo-diplomatic* model will require its ruling and opinions to carry authoritative weight in the arbitration and peacebuilding process and thus to ensure that its composition comprises the most respected authorities from the respective faith traditions to provide the added legitimacy and weight to the opinions that are formulated on pertinent matters of the conflict.

The checks and balances mechanism that are available via the *theo-diplomacy* model of conflict resolution increases the likelihood of resolving conflicts such as those seen in Kashmir, Palestine–Israel, and Afghanistan in an amicable manner, where the truce would be acceptable to the parties involved. For such a model to have the best chance of success, it is imperative that as part of the conflict resolution arbitrations framework, the body's authority, independence, neutrality, and ruling legitimacy is fully enshrined and respected by the parties involved in the conflict during in the negotiating process.

Finally, as I have shown, the *theo-diplomacy* paradigm is based on a key component in the Islamic model of peace and reconciliation, namely restorative justice, rather than retributive justice. This is lucidly expounded on in the following passage:

> "In Western retributive justice systems, it is expected that a person who commits a crime will be punished, but in Islamic restorative justice systems the aim is to repair the relationships that were broken by the conflict and heal the wounds that were caused by it." [407]

An example of restorative justice in practice is that of the Truth and Reconciliation Commission established in South Africa in 1996 at the end of apartheid. It was authorised by Nelson Mandela and chaired by Desmond Tutu. The victims of gross human rights violations gave statements about their experiences and the perpetrators of violence would give testimony and request amnesty from both civil and criminal prosecution with relative success. Such an interface is of paramount importance when looking to apply synergies between international and Islamic law, where the direction of travel and ethos of the diplomatic mission is orientated towards restorative justice rather than retribution subjugating the realpolitik machinations.

At the supranational level in the United Nations fora, the following reform recommendations would assist in the *theo-diplomacy* Peace and Reconciliation model for conflict resolution:

International Peace and Reconciliation Commission (IPRC) or Council is set up at the United Nations Security Council level comprising of leading religious and scholarly authorities from the major world religions.

The IPRC will be composed of leading representatives from Al-Azhar University, Qom Seminary, The Vatican, Chief Rabbinate Council, Anglican Communion, Protestant Communion, Sikh Gurdwaras and Hindu Temples to cite a few.

The IPRC will have representations from leading women from the respective faith-based communities and none promulgating and advocating the pivotal role that women can play in the peace and reconciliation process.

The role of the IPRC would be to act as a check and balance on state and non-state actors that are looking to use force against the sovereign integrity of another state on the pre-text that it is justified based on the principles of International Law, Islamic Law or the sacred traditions of the adherents.

For the IPRC to be effective, it will be imperative that the signatory states to the United Nations agree to submit to the jurisdiction of the IPRC with respect to the judgements that it makes.

An authoritative and fully functioning IPRC will look to clarify and counter those state and non-state actors that misconstrue and distort the principles of International Law and their sacred religious traditions to justify the use of force and aggression against other state, non-state actors and innocent civilians.

The IPRC will work towards achieving the UN Sustainable Development Goals (UNSDGs) such as *Quality Education* (UNSDG 4), *Gender Equality* (UNSDG 5), *Peace, Justice And Strong Institutions* (UNSDG 16).

In an age where the international rules-based order is being constantly challenged, it will be imperative that nation states that are signatories to the UN agree to adhere to the authority of the IPRC for it to have practical application and a chance of averting conflict in the first instance. For this to materialise, it is also imperative the political will is there from the parties involved to broker a peaceful resolution to a conflict as without this, the probability of achieving sustainable peace becomes more difficult.

To conclude, we note that Islamic law and international law have much in common—in their emphasis on core ideas such as peace, restoration and the resolution of conflict through dialogue. A comparative analysis of the two legal models shows that there are several meaningful points of convergence at play here. Furthermore, I have critically examined how the interplay between these two systems informs real-world conflict in Afghanistan, Palestine–Israel, and Kashmir. These sites of conflict tell us a great deal about the intersection between Islamic law and international law in the road to conflict resolution. Based on the findings of these contexts and a comparative analysis, this book has set the stage for an approach-based on *theo-diplomacy*. I have outlined the idea behind such a paradigm and have demonstrated, through examples and theory how this model has immense potential.

What is readily apparent is that the future pathways towards conflict resolution and peace and reconciliation will require practitioners in the field to be agile and well versed in the multi-faceted dimensions of the conventional and contemporary tools that are available at their disposal. If used with sincerity, supplemented with the political will that looks to neutralise the realpolitik machinations, these tools provide a meaningful opportunity for the doors of dialogue to open, for justice, sustainable peace and reconciliation to be realised in practice with a positive and long-lasting legacy to preserve our common humanity.

References

Ahmed al-Dawoody, "Islamic Law and International Humanitarian Law: An Introduction to the Main Principles," *International Review of the Red Cross,* Vol. 99, nb.3, (2017), 1018. untitled (icrc.org) (Accessed May 21st 2021).

Amnesty International, "Israel/OPT: Israel is committing apartheid, says UN Special Rapporteur." Amnesty International, March 23, 2022, https://www.amnesty.org/en/latest/news/2022/03/israel-opt-israel-is-committing-apartheid-says-un-special-rapporteur/ (Accessed June 30th 2022).

Ateek, Naim. "A Lecture Given by the Rev. Dr, Naim Ateek In Memory of Michael Prior." Palestinian Liberation Theology (2021), https://sabeel.org/wp-content/uploads/2021/12/Booklet-Summaries.pdf (Accessed June 30th 2022).

Ateek, N. S. *A Palestinian Theology of Liberation: The Bible, Justice, and the Palestine-Israel Conflict.* New York: Orbis, 2017.

Disasters Emergency Committee. "DEC raises £26m as 2022 signals 'unfolding catastrophe' in Afghanistan." Disasters Emergency Committee, December 29, 2021, DEC raises £26m as 2022 signals 'unfolding catastrophe' in Afghanistan | Disasters Emergency Committee (Accessed June 30th, 2022).

Fareed, Rifat. "What to Expect as Kashmir Leaders Meet India's Modi in New Delhi" for a synopsis of the parties involved in the Kashmir dispute." *Al Jazeera*, June 24, 2021,
What to expect as Kashmir leaders meet India's Modi in New Delhi | Conflict News | Al Jazeera (Accessed June 26, 2022).

Hayward, J. *"Justice, Jihad and Duty. The Qur'anic Concept of Armed Conflict."* Islam and Civilisational Renewal 9, No. 3 (2018): 267–303. *Islam and Civilisational Renewal, A journal devoted to contemporary issues and policy research,* Volume 9, Number 3, July 2018. Produced and distributed by *International Institute of Advanced Islamic Studies (IAIS) Malaysia.*

Hamza Yusuf, Shaykh. "Buddha in the Qur'an?" In *Common Ground Between Islam and Buddhism,* edited by Reza S. Kazemi. Jordan: Fons Vitae, The Royal Aal-Bayt Institute for Islamic Thought, 2010.

Hashim, A. and R. Fareed "Who are Kashmir's Armed Groups?" *Al Jazeera*, March 3, 2019, https://www.aljazeera.com/news/2019/3/3/explainer-who-are-kashmirs-armed-groups (Accessed, June 30, 2022)

J&K Tourism Development Corporation. "Religions in Kashmir," (2017), https://www.jktdc.co.in/religions-in-kashmir.aspx#:~:text=Christian,%25) and Christianity (0.3%25) (Accessed, June 30, 2022)

Mitchell, Andrew. *Beyond A Fringe: Tales from a Reformed Establishment Lackey*, Biteback Publishing Ltd, London, 2021.

Nasser Ishtayeh, NBC News. "Foreign governments stunned at Hamas victory." January 26, 2006. (Accessed June 27, 2022).

Newlines Institute, "The Uyghur Genocide: An Examination of China's Breaches of the 1948 Genocide Convention, March 8, 2021." https://newlinesinstitute.org/uyghurs/the-uyghur-genocide-an-examination-of-chinas-breaches-of-the-1948-genocide-convention/ (Accessed December 15, 2021).

Office of the United Nations High Commissioner for Human Rights. "Update of the Situation of Human Rights in Indian-Administered Kashmir and Pakistan-Administered Kashmir from May 2018 to April 2019." https://www.ohchr.org/sites/default/files/Documents/Countries/IN/KashmirUpdateReport_8July2019.pdf (Accessed December 16, 2021).

Payne, L. and Islamic Relief. *Introduction to Peacebuilding: An Islamic Relief Practitioners' Guide*. Stockholm: Islamic Relief Sweden, 2020. Introduction to Peacebuilding: An Islamic Relief Practitioners' Guide – World | ReliefWeb (Accessed December 17, 2021).

H.R.H. Prince Ghazi bin Muhammad, "A Common Word Between Us and You." 5-Year Anniversary Edition, MABDA English Monograph Series, No. 20, The Royal Aal Al Bayt Institute for Islamic Thought, 2012. 020-A-Common-Word-5th-Year.pdf (rissc.jo) (Accessed June 30, 2022).

Tariq Al-Thaqafi, *"Prominent Muslim Figures: Religious, cultural diversity does not justify "conflict." 31st May 2019.* Prominent Muslim figures: religious, cultural diversity does not justify 'conflict' | Arab News (Accessed December 19, 2021).

NOTES

[1] M. N. Shaw, *International Law*, 8th edn. (Cambridge: Cambridge University Press, 2017), 764.
[2] United Nations, *Charter of the United Nations*, 1945, https://www.un.org/en/about-us/un-charter/full-text (Accessed January 3, 2022).
[3] United Nations Charter, Chapter VI: Pacific Settlement of Disputes, Art.33, 1945. Chapter VI: Pacific Settlement of Disputes (Articles 33-38) | United Nations (Accessed January 3, 2002).
[4] In general, resolutions adopted by the Security Council acting under Chapter VII of the Charter are considered binding, in accordance with Article 25 of the Charter.
[5] United Nations Charter, Article 25.
[6] See further Sir H. Lauterpacht, *The Function of Law in the International Community* (Oxford, Oxford University Press, 2011).
[7] See examples of the Iranian Hostage Case: IJC Rep. 1980, 3, 22–23; 61 ILR, 530, 548–49. The Nicaragua case, see ICJ Rep. 1984, 392, 435–36; 76 ILR, 104, 146–47.
[8] United Nations Charter, Article 37(10).
[9] United Nations, *Vienna Convention on the Representation of States in their Relations with International Organizations of a Universal Character* (1975), https://legal.un.org/ilc/texts/instruments/english/conventions/5_1_1975.pdf (Accessed 30 January 2021).
[10] See further the *Manila Declaration on the Peaceful Settlement of International Disputes* (15 November 1982), https://cil.nus.edu.sg/wp-content/uploads/formidable/18/1982-Manila-Declaration-on-the-Peaceful-Settlement-of-International-Disputes.pdf (Accessed January 1, 2022). This document reaffirms the principles set out in the Charter that all States shall settle their disputes by peaceful means and listed, inter-alia, negotiation, mediation, and good offices as means to seek a peaceful settlement.
[11] David, D. Caron, "War and international adjudication: reflections on the 1899 peace conference," *American Journal of International Law* 94, no. 1 (2000): 4–30.
[12] See *1899 Hague Convention for the Pacific Settlement of International Disputes*, https://docs.pca-cpa.org/2016/01/1899-Convention-for-the-Pacific-Settlement-of-International-Disputes.pdf, specifically Article 9 (Accessed January 1, 2022).
[13] (S/2259,1991, para.20)
[14] Shaw, *International Law*, 925
[15] General Assembly Resolution 2626 (XXV), *Declaration on Principles of International Law concerning Friendly Relations and Co-operation among States in accordance with the Charter of the United Nations* (24 October 1970) UN Doc

A/RES/2625, https://digitallibrary.un.org/record/202170?ln=en (Accessed January 3, 2022).
[16] See further Article 33 (1) of the *United Nations Charter* and section 1 (3) and (10) of the *Manila Declaration*.
[17] United Nations, *Treaty on the Non-Proliferation of Nuclear Weapons (NPT)*, https://www.un.org/disarmament/wmd/nuclear/npt/text/ (Accessed January 3, 2022)
[18] Shaw, *International Law*, 770.
[19] General Assembly 43/51, *Declaration on the Prevention and Removal of Disputes and Situations Which May Threaten International Peace and Security and on the Role of the United Nations in This Field* (5 December 1988) UN Doc A/RES/43/51, https://www.refworld.org/docid/3b00f2274b.html (Accessed January 1, 2022). For Afghanistan 1988, the Geneva Agreements of that year specifically noted that a representative of the Secretary General would lend his good offices to the parties.
[20] *1899 Hague Convention* (n. 9).
[21] Shaw, *International Law,* 796.
[22] Shaw, *International Law*, 799. See Arbitration Commission on Yugoslavia, Interlocutory Decision, 4 July 1992, 92 IL 194, 197.
[23] Shaw, *International Law*, 800.
[24] Shaw, *International Law*, 801.
[25] M. Shahabuddeen, *Precedent in the World Court* (Cambridge: Cambridge University Press, 1996), 22.
[26] Art.2, Statute of the International Court of Justice, 1945, Statute of the Court | International Court of Justice (icj-cij.org), (Accessed 30 January, 2022).
[27] See Nuclear Tests Case, ICJ Reports, 1974, 253, 270–71; 57 ILR, 398, 415–16.
[28] See the Mavrommatis Palestine Concessions (Jurisdiction) case, PCIJ Series A, No.2, 1924, 11.
[29] ICJ Rep. 1950, 65, 74, ILR, 331, 336).
[30] Shaw, *International Law*, 811.
[31] Shaw, *International Law*, p. 936.
[32] See Summaries | Fisheries Jurisdiction (Spain v. Canada) | International Court of Justice (icj-cij.org), 4 Dec 1998.
[33] See the Genocide Convention (Bosnia v. Serbia) Case, ICJ Reports, 2007, 43, 91.
[34] Shaw, *International Law*, 941.
[35] Shaw, *International Law*, 817.
[36] Shaw, *International Law*, 942.
[37] Shaw, *International Law*, 942.
[38] https://opil.ouplaw.com/view/10.1093/law-mpeipro/e1575.013.1575/law-mpeipro-e1575 , Forum Prorogatum, Yaël Ronen.
[39] ICJ Rep. 2002, 303, 421.
[40] See further Shaw, International Law, 822.
[41] Shaw, *International Law*, 943.
[42] Article 36 (6) states as follows: In the event of a dispute as to whether the Court has jurisdiction, the matter shall be settled by the decision of the Court.
[43] Shaw, *International Law*, 947.
[44] Art 36 (2), *Statute of The International Court of Justice*, 1945, Statute of the Court | International Court of Justice (icj-cij.org) (Accessed 30 January, 2022).

[45] Shaw, *International Law*, 947.
[46] *Id.*
[47] ICJ Rep. 1998, 275.
[48] See ICJ Rep. 2004, 1307, 1351.
[49] ICJ Rep. 1966, 226; 110 ILR, 163.
[50] ICJ Report. 1996.226; 1 10 ILR, 163.
[51] Shaw, *International Law*, 827.
[52] Shaw, *International Law*, 829.
[53] Article 48 of the Statute; see Shaw, *International Law*, 954.
[54] See Nicaragua v. Honduras, ICJ Reports, 2007, 659, 695 and 697.
[55] Shaw, *International Law*, 838.
[56] Article 61 of the Statute.
[57] See The Legality of the Threat of Nuclear Weapons Case, ICJ Rep. 1996, 226, 236;110 ILR, 163.
[58] Art 96(2), Chapter XIV- The International Court of Justice, Charter of the United Nations, 1945. Chapter XIV: Article 96 — Charter of the United Nations — Repertory of Practice of United Nations Organs — Codification Division Publications (Accessed 31 December 2021).
[59] Shaw, *International Law*, 773.
[60] See Murty, "Settlement". Merrils notes that by 1940, nearly 200 conciliation treaties had been concluded: International Dispute Settlement, p.60.
[61] See *Vienna Convention on the Law of Treaties* (1969), https://legal.un.org/ilc/texts/instruments/english/conventions/1_1_1969.pdf (Accessed 31 December 2021).
[62] Shaw, *International Law*, 774.
[63] Art 15(1) of *1928 General Act on the Pacific Settlement of International Disputes* (revised in 1949). 1928-General-Act-of-Arbitration.pdf (nus.edu.sg) (Accessed 31 December 2021).
[64] Shaw, *International Law*, 774.
[65] Art 52(1) *Charter of the United Nations, 1945,* United Nations Charter (full text) | United Nations (Accessed 31 December 2021).
[66] See further. Charter of the United Nations, 1945, United Nations Charter (full text) | United Nations (Accessed 31 December 2021)
[67] Shaw, *International Law*, 848.
[68] See further ICJ Rep. 1986, 14.
[69] United Nations Charter, Article 2(4),
[70] General Assembly Resolution 2131 (XX), *Declaration on the Inadmissibility of Intervention in the Domestic Affairs of States and the Protection of Their Independence and Sovereignty* (21 December 1965), http://www.worldlii.org/int/other/UNGA/1965/124.pdf (Accessed January 3, 2022).
[71] General Assembly Resolution 2625 (n. 11).
[72] See further ICJ Rep. 1986, 14, 109–10; 76 ILR, 349, 443–44.
[73] Shaw, *International Law*, 861.
[74] Shaw, *International Law*, 862.
[75] See Daniel Webster, *Letter from U.S. Secretary of State Daniel Webster to British Minister Henry Fox* (24 April 1841), 29 BRrr. & FOR. ST. PAPERS 1137 (1841).

[76] See Daniel Webster, *Letter from U.S. Secretary of State Daniel Webster to British Minister Henry Fox* (24 April 1841), 29 BRrr. & FOR. ST. PAPERS 1137 (1841).
[77] Shaw, *International Law*, 868.
[78] Shaw, *International Law*, 864.
[79] United Nations Security Council, S/2001/946. *Letter dated 7 October 2001 from the Permanent Representative of the United States of America to the United Nations addressed to the President of the Security Council*. 2001 Letter dated 7 October 2001 from the Permanent Representative of the United States of America to the United Nations addressed to the President of the Security Council (Accessed January 1, 2022).
[80] 41 International Legal Materials (ILM), 2002, 1478.
[81] See C. Gray, "The Bush Doctrine Revisited: The 2006 National Security Strategy of the USA," *Chinese Journal of International Law* 5/3 (2006): 555.
[82] Shaw, *International Law*, 868. See e.g., General Assembly, *A More Secure World: Our Shared Responsibility. Report of the High-Level Panel on Threats, Challenges, and Change* (2 December 2004) UN Doc A/59/565, https://www2.ohchr.org/english/bodies/hrcouncil/docs/gaA.59.565_En.pdf (Accessed January 1, 2022); see also: General Assembly, *In Larger Freedom: Towards Development, Security, and Human Rights for All, Report of the Secretary General* (26 May 2005) UN Doc A/59/2005/Add.3, https://www.ohchr.org/Documents/Publications/A.59.2005.Add.3.pdf (Accessed January 1, 2022,), paragraph 125. Both state that where a threat is less than imminent, resort should be had to the Security Council.
[83] Shaw, *International Law*, 869.
[84] See Reality Check Team (BBC News), "Soleimani Attack: What does International Law Say?" BBC News, January 7, 2020, https://www.bbc.com/news/world-51007961 (Accessed December 31, 2021).
[85] BBC News "Soleimani Attack." See also the 2010 UN report on "targeted killings."
[86] See U.S. Department of Defence, Statement by the Department of Defense > U.S. Department of Defense > Release, Jan. 2, 2020 (Accessed January 3, 2022)
[87] See M. Hosenball, Trump says Soleimani plotted 'imminent' attacks, but critics question just how soon | Reuters, Jan 3, 2020. (Accessed January 3,2022).
[88] UN Report, 25, A/HRC/14/24/Add.6, Report of the Special Rapporteur on extrajudicial, summary or arbitrary executions, Philip Alston, see: https://www2.ohchr.org/english/bodies/hrcouncil/docs/14session/A.HRC.14.24.Add6.pdf.
[89] See BBC News "Soleimani Attack" on the Iraqi government's stance.
[90] United Nations Security Council, Resolution 502 (3 April 1982) UN Doc S/RES/502(1982), https://digitallibrary.un.org/record/34455?ln=en (Accessed January 3, 2022).
[91] Article 51; Shaw, *International Law*, 872
[92] *Ibid*.
[93] See General Assembly Resolution 2626 (n. 11) and General Assembly Resolution 3314 (XXIX), *Definition of Aggression* (14 December 1974),

https://legal.un.org/avl/pdf/ha/da/da_e.pdf (Accessed January 1, 2022). These referred ambiguously to the right of peoples entitled to, but forcibly deprived of, the right of self-determination to struggle to that end and to seek and receive support, in accordance with the principles of the Charter and in conformity with the 1970 declaration.

[94] *Art 2 (4) United Nations Charter, 1945,* United Nations Charter (full text) | United Nations (Accessed 3 December 2021).

[95] Shaw, *International Law*, 875.

[96] See P. M. McKinley, "Afghanistan's Looming Catastrophe," *Foreign Affairs* (3 December 2021), https://www.foreignaffairs.com/articles/afghanistan/2021-12-03/afghanistans-looming-catastrophe (Accessed January 1, 2022).

[97] G. Evans et al, *The Responsibility to Protect. Report of the International Commission on Intervention and State Sovereignty* (Ottawa: International Development Research Centre, 2001), https://undocs.org/pdf?symbol=en/a/57/303 (Accessed January 1, 2022,)

[98] General Assembly Resolution 3034, *Measures to Prevent International Terrorism* (18 December 1972) UN Doc A/RES/3034 (XXVII), https://unispal.un.org/DPA/DPR/unispal.nsf/85255db800470aa485255d8b004e349a/69cb600fbde9eddd852570840050c345?OpenDocument (Accessed January 1, 2022).

[99] Shaw, *International Law*, 888. See further Organisation for Security and Cooperation in Europe, *Action Against Terrorism*, www.osce.org/secretariat/terrorism (Accessed January 3, 2022).

[100] International Committee of the Red Cross, *Article 2: Application of the Convention*, https://ihl-databases.icrc.org/applic/ihl/ihl.nsf/Comment.xsp?action=openDocument&documentId=BE2D518CF5DE54EAC1257F7D0036B518 (Accessed January 3, 2022).

[101] *Convention (I) for the Amelioration of the Condition of the Wounded and Sick in Armed Forces in the Field, Geneva, 12 August 1949.* IHL Treaties - Geneva Convention (I) on Wounded and Sick in Armed Forces in the Field,1949 (icrc.org), See also updated ICRC Commentary on the First Geneva Convention published online in March 2016, IHL Treaties - Geneva Convention (I) on Wounded and Sick in Armed Forces in the Field,1949 - Commentary of 2016 Foreword | Foreword | Foreword (icrc.org) (Accessed January 3, 2022).

[102] *Art 43-Armed Forces,* IHL Treaties – Additional Protocol (I) to the Geneva Conventions, 1977 – Article 43 (icrc.org) *Article 44-Combatants and Prisoner of War, Geneva Conventions of 1949, Additional Protocols and their Commentaries:* - IHL Treaties - Additional Protocol (I) to the Geneva Conventions, 1977 - Article 44 (icrc.org) (Accessed January 3, 2022).

[103] Shaw, *International Law*, 897. See also, *The Economist*, the treatment of allied prisoners of war by Iraq in the 1991 Gulf War, 26 January 1991, 24 and the 2003 Gulf War: See also International Committee of the Red Cross (ICRC), *Report of the International Committee of the Red Cross (ICRC) on the Treatment by the Coalition Forces of Prisoners of War and Other Protected Persons by the Geneva Conventions in Iraq during Arrest, Internment, and Interrogation* published in February 2004,

https://cryptome.org/icrc-report.htm (Accessed January 1, 2022).

[104] *Art 3, Geneva Convention Relative to the Treatment of Prisoners of War,* 12 August 1949- Geneva Convention relative to the Treatment of Prisoners of War | OHCHR (Accessed January 1, 2022).

[105] *Art 4, Geneva Convention Relative to the Treatment of Prisoners of War,* 12 August 1949, Geneva Convention relative to the Treatment of Prisoners of War | OHCHR (Accessed January 1, 2022). See also *Convention (IV) respecting the Laws and Customs of War on Land and its annex: Regulations concerning the Laws and Customs of War on Land. The Hague, 18 October 1907.* IHL Treaties - Hague Convention (IV) on War on Land and its Annexed Regulations, 1907 (icrc.org) (Accessed January 1, 2022).

[106] *Art.43 Hague Regulations:* IHL Treaties - Hague Convention (II) on the Laws and Customs of War on Land, 1899 - Regulations: Art. 43 (icrc.org) (Accessed January 1, 2022).

[107] See *International Court of Justice, Legal Consequences of the Construction of a Wall in the Occupied Palestinian Territory Advisory Opinion No. 2004/28, 9 July 2004,* 131-20040709-PRE-01-00-EN.pdf (icj-cij.org) (Accessed January 1, 2022).

[108] African Commission on Human and Peoples' Rights, "Legal instruments," https://achpr.org/legalinstruments/detail?id=10.

[109] See further *Hassan v. The United Kingdom,* European Court of Human Rights, Grand Chamber, Application no. 29750/09, Judgment, Strasbourg, 16 September 2014, http://hudoc.echr.coe.int/sites/eng (Accessed January 1, 2022), para 101ff. See also R. Goodman, "Authorization versus Regulation of Detention in Non-International Armed Conflicts," *International Law Studies* 91 (2015): 155.

[110] ICJ Rep. 2015, paras. 151 ff.

[111] Shaw, *International Law,* 905.

[112] Shaw, *International Law,* 907.

[113] ICJ Rep. 1996, 226, 257 and 252.

[114] ICJ Rep, 1986, p.247.

[115] Ibid, p.248.

[116] E.g. Such as the Peace Treaties of 10 February 1947, The Nuclear Test Ban Treaty, 1963, the Nuclear Non-Proliferation Treaty, 1968 (extended indefinitely in 1995) to cite a few.

[117] ICJ Rep. 1996, pp. 254-5.

[118] ICJ Rep. 1996, pp. 254–55.

[119] United Nations Security Council, Resolution 984 (11 April 1995) UN Doc S/RES/984(1995), https://digitallibrary.un.org/record/176507?ln=en (Accessed January 3, 2022). See also Shaw, *International Law,* 910.

[120] Shaw, *International Law,* 911.

[121] International Committee of the Red Cross (ICRC), *Geneva Convention Relative to the Protection of Civilian Persons in Time of War (Fourth Geneva Convention)* 75 UNTS 287 (12 August 1949), https://www.refworld.org/docid/3ae6b36d2.html (Accessed January 1, 2022,). See J. Pictet, Commentary on the Geneva Conventions of 12 August 1949, Geneva 1952, Vol. 1, 29. See also Tadic' case, IT-94-1, Decision on jurisdiction, para. 70, 105, ILR, 453, 488.

[122] See Tadic' case, IT-94-1, Decision on jurisdiction, para. 70, 105, ILR, 453, 488. Case No. IT-94-1-AR 72; 105 ILR, pp. 453, 486 ff.
[123] Tadic Case No. IT-94-1-AR; 105, ILR, 453, 506.
[124] Art. 3, Geneva Convention Relative to the Treatment of Prisoners of War, 12 August 1949, Geneva Convention relative to the Treatment of Prisoners of War | OHCHR (Accessed January 3, 2022).
[125] ICJ Rep. 1986, 3, 114; 76 ILR, 349, 448.
[126] Art. 3, Genevan Convention Relative to the Treatment of Prisoners of War, 12 August 1949, Geneva Convention relative to the Treatment of Prisoners of War | OHCHR (Accessed January 3, 2022).
[127] Shaw, *International Law*, 917.
[128] *Art.4, United Nations International Covenant on Civil and Political Rights, 16 December 1966, General Assembly Resolution 2200A (XXI)*, International Covenant on Civil and Political Rights | OHCHR (Accessed January 3, 2022).
[129] *Art.27, United Nations International Covenant on Civil and Political Rights, 16 December 1966, General Assembly Resolution 2200A (XXI)*, International Covenant on Civil and Political Rights | OHCHR (Accessed January 3, 2022).
[130] See *Letter dated 95/01/05 the Permanent Representative of Norway and the Chargé d'Affaires of the Permanent Mission of Finland addressed to the Commission on Human Rights*, E/CN.4/1995/116 (1995), https://digitallibrary.un.org/record/226914?ln=en (Accessed January 1, 2022); Office of the High Commissioner for Human Rights, *Minimum Humanitarian Standards*, E/CN.4/RES/1995/29, https://ap.ohchr.org/documents/alldocs.aspx?doc_id=4304 (Accessed January 1, 2022); United Nations Economic and Social Council, *Effective Functioning of Bodies Established Pursuant to United Nations Human Rights Instruments*, E/CN.4/1995/81, https://documents-dds-ny.un.org/doc/UNDOC/GEN/G94/750/98/PDF/G9475098.pdf?OpenElement (Accessed January 1, 2022); See also T. Meron and A. Rosas, "A Declaration of Minimum Humanitarian Standards," *American Journal of International Law* 85/2 (2017): 375–77.
[131] See Declaration for the Protection of War Victims, 1993, A/48/742 Final declaration of the International Conference for the Protection of War Victims - ICRC
[132] See International Committee of the Red Cross (ICRC), *International Review of the Red Cross* 272 (Sept.–Oct. 1989): 404, https://international-review.icrc.org/reviews/irrc-no-272-international-review-red-cross-10-1989 (Accessed January 3, 2022).
[133] Peter R. Kyle, Rotary International Director prefers to use the terms "Peacebuilding" than "Peace." "Peacebuilding: It's In Our DNA," https://www.bing.com/videos/search?q=Peter+R+Kyle+Peacebuilding+in+our+DNA&docid=607999371666862976&mid=0C8C942CB6E8F068F61C0C8C942CB6E8F068F61C&view=detail&FORM=VIRE (Accessed March 2, 2021).
[134] Khaled Abou El Fadl, *Reasoning With God. Reclaiming Shari'ah in the Modern Age* (Washington, DC: Rowman and Littlefield, 2014), xxxii.
[135] See S. S. Ali, *Modern Challenges to Islamic Law* (Cambridge: Cambridge University Press, 2019), 20–22.
[136] El Fadl, *Reasoning With God*, xxxii.

[137] Khaled Abou El Fadl, Atif Ahmed, and Fares Hassan, eds., *Routledge Handbook of Islamic Law* (London and New York: Taylor and Francis), 705.

[138] Khaled Abou El Fadl, "The Shari'ah." In *The Oxford Handbook of Islam ana Politics*. Oxford Islamic Studies Online, http://www.oxfordislamicstudies.com/article/opr/t9001/e041 (Accessed January 8, 2022).

[139] Qur'an 89: 27–28. This is also used with reference to the companions of the Prophet (where they are pleased with God and God is pleased with them).

[140] The "Prophet" here is Muhammad, the final Messenger of God, according to the Islamic tradition. "Allah" is the name of "God" in Islam. Note: in the hadith, one finds after Muhammad's name or title the words "prayers and peace be upon him" (represented in calligraphy (ﷺ) as a mark of respect and reverence. This calligraphy is not used throughout this book but can be implied where the name Muhammad is cited.

[141] J. M. Cowan, ed., *The Hans Wehr Dictionary of Modern Written Arabic* (New York: BN Publishing, 1999), 496.

[142] Qur'an, 8:61.

[143] Qur'an, 2:182.

[144] Cited in Bukhari al Sahih, 3: 1090, 2827, Muslim in al-Sahih, 2:699, 1009, Ahmad b. Hanbal in al-Musnad, 2:316, 8168.

[145] Qur'an, 2:224.

[146] Qur'an, 4:114.

[147] Note that although "brothers" is used in this description, the same can be applied for "sisters" i.e. (all) believers are "sisters" (to one another).

[148] Qur'an, 49:9–10.

[149] Cited in Bukhari in al Sahih, 2:958, 2546, Muslim in al-Sahih 4:2011, 2605, Ahmad b. Hanbal in al-Musnad, 6:403, 27313.

[150] Cited in Abu Dawud in al-Sunan, 4:280, 4920. Al-Tirmidhi in al-Sunan, 4:331, 1938. Abd al-Razzaq in al-Musnannaf, 11:158, 20196.

[151] Cited in Abu Dawud in al-Sunan, 4:280, 4920.

[152] Cited in Bukhari in al Tarikh al-Kabir, 3:295, 1007, al-Quda'I in Musnad al-Shihab, 2:244, 1280, Abd b. Humayd in al-Musnad, 1:135, 335.

[153] Cited in al-Tabarani in al-Mu'jam al-Kabir, 8:257, 7999. Al- Tayalisi in al-Musnad, 1:81, 598. Al-Bayhaqi in Shu'ab al-Iman, 7:490, 11094. Al-Dhahabi in al-Kabair, p.212. Al-Haythami in al-Majma al-Zawaid, 8:80.

[154] Cited by Abu Nu'aym in Hilyat al-Awliya, 8:112.

[155] Qur'an, 4:29-30. Note-"Him" can also imply "Her" as the principle being discussed applies to both genders.

[156] Qur'an, 5:32.

[157] Al-Lubab fi ulum al-Kitab (7:301).

[158] Al-Hasan al Basri (642 CE- 728 CE) was a leading Muslims theologian, ascetic, mystic, scholar and jurist who belonged to second generation of Muslims coming after the first generation which featured the direct companions of the Prophet Muhammad.

[159] Qur'an, 17:33.

[160] Cited in Muslim in The Book of Piety, Filial Duty and Good Manners, chapter: "On the Prohibition of Pointing a Weapon at Someone Else" (al-Hakim).

[161] Cited in Muslim-The Book of Piety, Filial Duty and Good Manners, chapter "On the Prohibition of Pointing a Weapon at Someone Else", 4:2020, 2617, al-Hakim in Mustadrak, 3:587, al-Bayhaqi in al-Sunan al-Kubra, 8:23, 2617.

[162] Cited in al-Bukhari, The Book of Taxation for Non-Muslims Living in an Islamic State, The Sin of Someone Who Kills a Non-Muslim Citizen Without His Having Committed a Crime", 3:1155. 2995. Ibn Majah in The Book of Blood Money, "Someone Who Kills a Non-Muslim Citizen," 2:896, 2686, al-Bazzar in al Musnad, 6:368, 2383.

[163] Cited in al-Nisa'I in The Book of Taking an Oath], "The Enormity of Murdering a Non-Muslim Citizen," 8:25.

[164] "The Enormity of Murdering a Non-Muslim Citizen," 63: See further narration by al-Bukhari in al-Sahih: Kitab al Maghazi {The Book of Military Expeditions]: "The Blessed Prophet's Sending of Usama b. Zayd to the Campsites of the juhayna Tribe," 4:1555 .4021.

[165] Narrated by Muslim in al-Sahih: Kitab al-Iman [The Book of Faith], chapter: On Prohibition of Killing a a person of no faith when He Says, "There is no god but God." 1:97 .94-97.

[166] It is important to set out the modalities of the principle of no faith. There is a person of no faith who has not been invited to Islam, nor had the faith explained to them. There are no repercussions for such a person in the Islamic tradition. There is a person of no faith who has been invited to Islam and has had the teachings explained but who, despite understanding them, decides not to accept or embrace Islam. Classical jurists have also used the phrase "Ummate Dawat," i.e., those people who have been invited to Islam and have not accepted it, and "Ummate Ijabat," i.e., those people who have been given the invitation of Islam and have accepted and embraced it based on their own free will without compulsion.

[167] Narrated by al-Bukhari in al Sahih: Kitab al Maghazi [The Book of Military Expeditions], chapter: "On the Angels Being Present at the Battle of Badr", 4:1474 .3794; and Muslim in al-Sahih: Kitab al-Iman [The Book of Faith], chapter: "On the Prohibition of Killing a Disbeliever when He Says, "There is no god but God.", 1:95 .95.

[168] Cited by Ibn Majah in al-Sunan: Kitab al-Diyat [The Book of Blood Money], chapter: The Gravity of Unjustly Killing a Muslim, 2:874 .2620; al-Rabi in al-Musnad, I:368 .960; and al-Bayhaqi in Sunan al Kubra, 8:22 .15646.

[169] Qur'an, 85:10.

[170] Al-Razi, al-Tafsir al Kabir, 13: III.

[171] Al-Razi, al-Tafsir al-Kabir, 3I:111.

[172] Qur'an, 2:195.

[173] Qur'an, 4:29–30.

[174] Al-Razi, al-Tafsir al-Kabir, 10:57.

[175] Narrated by al-Bukhari in al-Sahih: Kitab al-tibb [The Book of Medicine], "Taking Poison and Using it for Medical Treatment, or Using What May be Dangerous or Impure", 5: 2179 ,5442.

[176] Muslim in al-Sahih: Kitab al-Iman [The Book of Faith], The Strict Forbiddance of Killing Oneself, and if someone commits suicide with something, he will be tormented with the same in the hellfire", 1:104 .110.

[177] Narrated by Muslim in Sahih: Kitab al-imara [The Book of Leadership], chapter: "The Obligation to Obey the Leaders", 3:1469 .1840. In this situation an Ansar leader had started a fire and was instructing his followers as part of his military garrison to "enter it." Some were about to enter whilst other said that "we are free of it as we embraced Islam to avoid the fire." The Prophet stated, "if they entered it, they would have remained in it until the day of resurrection."

[178] Narrated by al-Bukhari in al-Sahih: Kitab. Principle applies to both a man and a woman.

[179] Qur'an 5:32.

[180] Narrated by al-Bukhari in al-Sahih: Kitab al Hajj [The Book of Pilgrimage], chapter: "The Sermon During the Days of Mina", 2:620 .1654; and Muslim in al-Sahih, 3:1305-1306 .1679.

[181] Qur'an, 5:8.

[182] Qur'an, 60:8.

[183] Cited in Muslim, in al Sahih: Kitab al Jihad wa al-Siyar [The Book of Martial Jihad and Battles], 3:1444 .1812.

[185] Narrated by Malik in al-Muwatta: Kitab al-Jihad [The Book of Martial Jihad], chapter: "The Unlawfulness of Killing Women and Children During Military Expeditions, 2:447 4965.

[186] Cited in Malik in al-Muwatta, 2:448 . 966. Abd al-Razzaq in al-Musannaf, 5:199, al-Bayhaqi in al Sunan al Kubra, 9:85.

[187] Cited in al-Hindi, Kanz al-Ummal, 4:474, .11409.

[188] Al-Qurafi, al-Furuq, 3:29.

[189] Ibn al Qayyum, Ahkam ahl al-dhimma, I:165, Ibn Qudama al-Maqsidi, al-Mughani, 9:251.

[190] Cited in Abu Dawud in al-Sunan: Kitab al Jihad [The Book of Martial Jihad], Chapter: The Killing of Women; 3:53 . 2669; Ibn Majah in al-Sunan: Kitab al Jihad [The Book of Martial Jihad], 2:948 .2842; Ahmad b. Hanbal in al-Musnad, 3:488 . 16035; al-Nisai in al al-Sunan al Kubra, 5:186-187 ..8625, 8627, and al-Hakim al-Mustadrak, 2:133 . 2565.

[191] Cited in Muslim in al-Sahih: Kitab al-jihad wa al-siyar [The Book of Martial Jihad and Military Expeditions], "The Conquest of Mecca; 3:1407 .1780; Abu Dawud in al Sunan: Kitab al-Kharaj wa al-imara wa al fay" [The Book of Land Tax, Leadership and the Spoils Acquired without Fighting) 3:162 .3021; and al-Bazzar in al-Musnad, 4:122 .1292.

[192] Narrated by "Abd-al-Razzaq in al-Musannaf, 10: 124 .18591.

[193] Narrated by al Bukhari in al-Sahih: Kitab al-Maghazi [The Book of Military Expeditions], chapter: "The Campaign of Khaybar", 4:1538 .3961; Muslim in al-Sahih: Kitabl al-jihad wa al-siyar [The Book of Marital Jihad and Expeditions], Chapter "The Campaign of Khaybar", 3:1427 . 1365.

[194] Narrated by Abu Dawud in al-Sunan: Kitab al-Jihad [The Book of Martial Jihad, chapter: "The Abhorrence of Burning the Enemy; 3:55 .2675.

[195] Narrated by Abu Dawud in al-Sunan: Kitab al Kharaj wa al-imara wa al fay" [The Book of Land Tax, Leadership and the Spoils Acquired without Fighting], 3:170 .3050 al-Bayhaqi in al al-Sunan al Kubra, 9:204 .18508; and cited b Ibn Abd al-Barr in al-Tamhid, 1:149.

[196] Narrated by Abu Dawud in al-Sunan: Kitab al-jihad [The Book of Marital Jihad], 3:41 . 2629.

[197] Narrated by al-Tirmidhi in al-Sunan: Kitab al siyar [The Book of Military Expeditions], 4:122 .1552.

[198] Narrated by al-Marwazi in Musnad Abi Bakr, pp. 69-72 .21.

[199] The famous example of the fourth Caliph, Hazrat Ali, who did kill an opponent during battle after being antagonised. If he had done so, the response would have been deemed disproportionate, and in rage, which would go against the balanced disposition that the Islamic tradition teaches and upholds.

[200] Narrated by Ahmad b. Hanbal in al-Musnad, I:390 .3708.

[201] N Badawi, Islamic Jurisprudence and the Regulation of Armed Conflict, February 2009, Harvard University, https://reliefweb.int/sites/reliefweb.int/files/resources/8FC97823516EEEDA49257 62E001ABDA8-Harvard_Feb2009.pdf, 3 (Accessed January 8th, 2022)

[202] Ibid, 4.

[203] Ibid.

[204] Ibid, 5.

[205] Ibid, 7. *Fitna*- implies a major disputation that is causing major discord and strife amongst individuals-groups.

[206] El Fadl, *Rebellion and Violence*, 253.

[207] El Fadl, *Rebellion and Violence*, 856–66.

[208] El Fadl, *Rebellion and Violence*, 923–27.

[209] Qur'an: 49:9.

[210] El Fadl, *Rebellion and Violence*, 1848–50.

[211] *The Glorious Qur'an*, translated by Shaykh ul Islam Dr Muhammad Tahir ul Qadri (Minhaj al-Quran, 2012), The Table Spread Al-Ma'ida. 5:33, 34.

[212] El Fadl, Ahmed and Hassan, *Routledge Handbook of Islamic Law*.

[213] El Fadl, Ahmed and Hassan, *Routledge Handbook of Islamic Law*, 705.

[214] El Fadl, Ahmed and Hassan, *Routledge Handbook of Islamic Law*, 850.

[215] El Fadl, Ahmed and Hassan, *Routledge Handbook of Islamic Law*, 932.

[216] See E. J. Powell, Islamic Law and International Law *and International Law: Peaceful Resolution of Disputes* (Oxford: Oxford University Press, 2020), (Kindle edition), 86

[217] International Court of Justice, *Statute of the International Court of Justice*, https://www.icj-cij.org/en/statute (Accessed January 3, 2022,).

[218] See Powell, *Islamic Law and and International Law*, 101.

[219] Powell, Islamic Law and International Law,102–03.

[220] Powell, Islamic Law and International Law, 88.

[221] Awn Shawkat Al Khasawneh in Powell, Islamic Law and International Law,88.

[222] Powell, Islamic Law and International Law, 89.

[223] Sheikh Wahbeh al-Zuhli, *Islam and International Law, Vol 87, No. 858, June 2005, 278*. Islam and international law (icrc.org) (Accessed January 3, 2022).

[224] Powell, Islamic Law and International Law, 92 cited from Badr, Gamal Moursi, *A Survey of Islamic International Law, Proceedings of the Annual Meeting,* American Society of International Law, 76 (April 22-24): 55-61.

[225] Powell, *Islamic Law and International Law*, 103.

[226] Powell, *Islamic Law and International Law*, 93.

[227] James L. Brierly. "The Law of Nations: An Introduction to the International Law of Peace," Sixth Edition, Edited by Sir Humphrey Waldock, Oxford University Press, 1963. See also Andrew Clapham, "Brierly's Law of Nations, Seventh Edition. Oxford University Press, 2012.

[228] Powell, *Islamic Law and International Law*, 94.

[229] Powell, *Islamic Law and International Law*. 94.

[230] Powell, *Islamic Law and International Law*. 94.

[231] See further Juan Cole, "Muhammad and Justinian: Roman Legal Traditions and the Qur'ān," *Journal of Near Eastern Studies* 79 no. 2 (2020): 183–96.

[232] Powell, Islamic Law and International Law, p 84.

[233] Powell, *Islamic Law and International Law*.

[234] Powell, Islamic Law and International Law,95-citing Rosenne, Shabtai, 1999, 65. *The Influence of Judaism on the Development of International Law, in* Mark W. Janis and Carolyn Evans, *eds, Religion and International Law, 63-94. The Hague, the Netherlands: Kluwer Law International.*

[235] Hugo Grotius, *On the Law of War and Peace* (Cambridge: Cambridge University Press, 2012).

[236] Powell, Islamic Law and International Law, 96

[237] Powell, Islamic Law and International Law, 97.

[238] See David Armstrong, Theo Farrell and Helen Lambert, *International Law and International Relations,* Second Edition, Cambridge University Press, 2012, 61.

[239] Christine Chinkin and Mary Kaldor, *International Law And New Wars, Cambridge University Press, 2017, 67.*

[240] Powell, *Islamic Law and International Law*, 115.

[241] Gavcikovo-Nagymaros Project (Hungry v. Slovakia), ICJ Judgement of September 25, 1997, ICJ REP 1997, 7; and North Sea Continental Shelf Cases (Federal Republic of Germany v. Denmark; Federal Republic of Germany v Netherlands), ICJ Judgement of Feb 20, 1969, ICJ Rep 1969, 3.

[242] Powell, *Islamic Law and International Law*,116. See also Antonio Casesse, *International Law*, Second Edition, Oxford University Press, 2005, 166.

[243] Hallaq, Wael B. 2009b. Sharia: Theory Practice Transformations, Cambridge, UK, Cambridge University Press, 71.

[244] For a discussion on Dicey's conception of the rule of law, see Albert Venn Dicey, *Lectures Introductory to the Study of the Law of the Constitution.* No. 43445-43449 London: Macmillan. 1885).

[245] Dicey, *Lectures Introductory*, 118.

[246] Qur'an, 16:91

[247] Rosen, Lawrence, *The Justice of Islam,* Oxford, UK; Oxford University Press, 2000, 11.

[248] *Art.53, Vienna Convention on the Law of Treaties 1969, Treaties Conflicting with a peremptory norm of general international law ("jus cogens"),* Vienna Convention on the Law of Treaties (1969) (un.org) (Accessed January 3, 2022).

[249] Powell, *Islamic Law and International Law*, 116.

[250] Ahmed al-Dawoody, "Islamic Law and International Humanitarian Law: An Introduction to the main principles", *International Review of the Red Cross*, vol. 99 (3), (2017), 999. See also Muhammad ibn Ahmad al-Sarakhsi, Kitab al-Mabsut, Vol. 10, Dar al-Ma'rifah, Beirut, 1986, p2.

[251] Leslie C. Green, The Contemporary Law of Armed Conflict, Melland Schill Studies in International Law, Third Edition, Manchester University Press, 2014.

[252] See further Rudolph F. Peters, *Jihad in Classical and Modern Islam* (Princeton, NJ: Markus Wiener, 1996), 119; Khaled Abou El Fadl, "The Rules of Killing at War: An Inquiry into Classical Sources," *The Muslim World*, 89/2 (April 1999): 150; Khaled Abou El Fadl, "Islam and the Theology of Power," *Middle East Report* 221 (2001): 30.; A. E. Mayer, "War and Peace in the Islamic Tradition and International Law," in *Just War and Jihad: Historical and Theoretical Perspectives on War and Peace in Western and Islamic Traditions*, eds. J.T. Johnson and J. Kelsay (Westport: Greenwood Press, 1991), 197; Sohail H. Hashmi, "Saving and Taking Life in War: Three Modern Muslim Views", *The Muslim World* 89/2 (1999): 158.

[253] Deuteronomy 20:19-20.

[254] See generally Lionel Giles, The Art of War, by Sun Tzu, The Project Gutenberg eBook, May 1994 (updated December 28, 2005), The Art of War (utoledo.edu) (Accessed January 1, 2022)

[255] al-Dawoody, "Islamic Law," 1001.

[256] Powell, *Islamic Law and International Law*, 19.

[257] Republic of the Maldives, *Constitution of the Maldives* (2008), Accessed January 1, 2022, https://www.constituteproject.org/constitution/Maldives_2008?lang=en

[258] Powell, *Islamic Law and International Law*, 98.

[259] Shaw, Malcolm N. *International Law*, Cambridge UK, Cambridge University Press, 2003, 12.

[260] Weiss, Bernard G, *The Spirit of Islamic Law*, Athens, University of Georgia Press, 2006, 116.

[261] An-Nai'im, Abdullahi Ahmed, Islam and the Secular State: Negotiating the Future of Shari'a. Cambridge, MA: Harvard University Press, 2008, 164.

[262] Bassiouni M. Cherif, *The Shari'a and Islamic Criminal Justice in Time of War and Peace*, New York, Cambridge University Press, 2014, 23.

[263] Qur'an, 59:7-*And whatever the Messenger gives you, take that and whatever he forbids you, abstain (from that).*

[264] Powell, *Islamic Law and International Law*, 123–24.

[265] Brotherhood and sisterhood can be implied here in an intertwined way.

[266] See generally Powell, Islamic Law and International Law, 7.

[267] Powell, *Islamic Law and International Law,* 7–8.

[268] Powell, *Islamic Law and International Law,* 10.

[269] Powell, *Islamic Law and International Law*, 78.

[270] Powell, *Islamic Law and International Law*, 80.

[271] Powell, *Islamic Law and International Law*, 78

[272] Powell, *Islamic Law and International Law*, 98.
[273] Powell, *Islamic Law and International Law*, 111.
[274] Powell, *Islamic Law and International Law*, 12.
[275] Powell, *Islamic Law and International Law*, 24.
[276] Powell, *Islamic Law and International Law*, 33-34. Powell interview with Imam Ibrahim Amin, Oxford Centre for Islamic Studies, Oxford, UK, May 16, 2016.
[277] Al Ghunami, Mohammad Talat, *The Muslim Conception of International Law and the Western Approach*, The Hague, the Netherlands, 1968, 95.
[278] Powell, *Islamic Law and International Law*, 42.
[279] Powell, *Islamic Law and International Law*, 46-47.
[280] See Shuaib, Farid, *The Islamic Legal System in Malaysia*, Pacific Rim Law and Policy Journal, 21 (1), 2012, 85-113.
[281] Weiss, Bernard G, *The Spirit of Islamic Law*, Athens, University of Georgia Press, 2006, 122.
[282] Narrated by al-Bayhaqi in al-Sunan al-Kubra, 9:83; Malik in al-Muwatta, 2:448, 966; Abd al-Razzaq in al-Musannaf, 5:199, 9375; al-Hindi in Kanz al-Ummal, 1:296; and cited by Ibn Qudama in al-Mughni, 8:451-452,477.
[283] Qur'an, trans. al Qudri, 2:205.
[284] International Committee of the Red Cross, "Protection of the Civilian Population," https://www.icrc.org/en/doc/what-we-do/protecting-civilians/overview-protection-civilian-population.htm.
[285] See further 'Alı ibn 'Umar al-Dāraqutnı, Sunan al-Dāraqutnı, eds. Sha 'ıb al-Arnu 'ūd, Ḥassan 'Abd al-Muna'm Shalabıand Sa'id al-Laḥām, Vol. 5, Mu'assasah al-Risālah (Beirut, 2004), 204. 48 Aḥmad ibn 'Alıibn Hajar al-'Asqalānı,Fatḥ al-BārıSharḥ Ṣaḥıh al-Bukhārı, ed. Muh yıal-Dın al-Khat ıb, Vol. 6, Dār al-Ma'rifah, (Beirut), 283. 49 W. al-Zuḥaylı, above note 19, p. 495. 50 'A. Ibn Ḥazm, above note 35, Vol. 5, 117. 51 M. al-Shaybānı, above note 25, Vol. 1, 79. 52 Ibid., Vol. 1, 79. A. Al-Dawoody.
[286] See Muḥammad ibn Jarır al-T abarı, Tārıkh al-T abarı: Ta rıkh al-Umam wa al-Mulu k, Vol. 2, Dār al-Kutub al'Ilmiyyah (Beirut, 2001), 39. Qur'an 47:4. 55 Qur'an 9:5. 56 Yūsuf al-Qaraḍāwı, Fiqh al-Jihād: Dirāsah Muqāranah li-Aḥkāmih wa Falsafatih fiḌaw' al-Qur'ān wa alSunnah, Vol. 2, Maktabah Wahbah (Cairo, 2009), 854 ff.; Muḥammad Ḥammıdulla h, *Muslim Conduct of State: Being a Treatise on Siyar, That is Islamic Notion of Public International Law, Consisting of the Laws of Peace, War and Neutrality, Together with Precedents from Orthodox Practice and Preceded by a Historical and General Introduction*, rev. and enl. 5th ed. (Sh. Muhammad Ashraf, Lahore, 1968), 214; Lena Salaymeh, "Early Islamic Legal-Historical Precedents: Prisoners of War," *Law and History Review* 26, no. 3, (2008): 528. 57 See 'Abd Allah ibn Maḥmūd ibn Mawdūd, Al-Ikhtiyār li-Ta'lıl al-Mukhta r, ed. 'Abd al-Latıf Muh ammad 'Abd al-Raḥman, 3rd ed., Vol. 4, Dār al-Kutub al-'Ilmiyyah, Beirut, 2005, p. 133; S. Mahmassani, above note 44 in text, 307.
[287] Id.
[288] See Muḥammad al-Khatıb al-Shirb ını,Mughnıal-Muḥtāj ilāMa'rifah Ma'ānıAlfāz' al-Minhāj, Vol. 4, Dār al-Fikr (Beirut), 237; 'A. Ṣaqr, above note 22, 83; al-Qaraḍāwı, Fiqh al-Jihād, 1178. 74 AP I, Art. 41(2)(b). 75 M. al-Shirbını, above note 73, p. 237 76 See ibid., 237; al-Dawoody, "Islamic Law," 132. 77 Muwaffaq al-Dın

'Abd Allah ibn Aḥmad ibn Qudāmah, Al-KāfifiFiqh al-Imām Aḥmad ibn Ḥanbal, ed. Muḥammad Fāris and Musʻad ʻAbd al-Ḥamıd al-Sa ʻdanı, Vol. 4, Da r al-Kutub al-ʻIlmiyyah, Beirut, 2004, p. 163. 78 Qur'an 17:70.

[289] See Jean-Marie Henckaerts and Louise Doswald-Beck, eds., *Customary International Humanitarian Law, Vol. 1: Rules* (Cambridge: Cambridge University Press, 2005), 406–09; Z. al-Zayd, above note 68 in text, pp. 49, 78; A. Abūal-Wafā, above note 62 in text, 206–09.

[290] See further www.muslimheritage.com

[291] Powell, *Islamic Law and International Law*, 126–27.

[292] Powell, *Islamic Law and International Law*, 131.

[293] Powell, *Islamic Law and International Law*, 133.

[294] Powell, *Islamic Law and International Law*. 133.

[295] Powell, *Islamic Law and International Law*, 134.

[296] Powell, *Islamic Law and International Law*, 136.

[297] Yusuf Abdulaqawi, *Diversity of Legal Traditions and International Law: Keynote Address, Cambridge Journal of International and Comparative Law*, 2 (4), 2013; 684.

[298] Powell, Islamic Law and International Law, 137.

[299] Powell, Islamic Law and International Law, 138.

[300] Hashmi, Sohail H. *Interpreting the Islamic Ethics of War and Peace. In Sohail. H. Hashmi, ed., Islamic Political Ethics: Civil Society, Pluralism, and Conflict, Princeton, NJ: Princeton University Press, 197.* Qur'an 2:208.

[301] Remarks by His Majesty King Abdullah II at the International Court of Justice, Royal Hashemite Court, King Abdullah II Official Website, October 31, 2006. Remarks by His Majesty King Abdullah II At the International Court of Justice | Royal Hashemite Court (rhc.jo) (Accessed January 2, 2021).

[302] Powell, Islamic Law and International Law, 142.

[303] Powell interview with Dr. Aida Othman, August 28, 2015, cited in Powell, *Islamic and International Law*, 142.

[304] Powell, *Islamic Law and International Law*, 143

[305] Powell, *Islamic Law and International Law*. 143.

[306] Powell, *Islamic Law and International Law*, 144.

[307] Goertz, Gary, Paul F. Diehl, and Alexandru Balas, *The Evolution of Peace in International System, Oxford, Oxford University Press, 2016, 172.*

[308] *Conciliation Commission on the Continental Shelf area between Iceland and Jan Mayen: Report and recommendations to the governments of Iceland and Norway, decision of June 1981,* Volume XXVII, 1-34. (Accessed January 2, 2021).

[309] Hashmi, Sohail H, *Islamic Ethics in International Society.* In Sohail H. Hashmi, ed, *Islamic Political Ethics: Civil Society, Pluralism, and Conflict, Princeton, Princeton University Press, 2002, 196.*

[310] Abou El Fadl, Khaled. *Conflict Resolution as a Normative Value in Islamic Law: Handling Disputes with Non-Muslims.* In Douglas Johnson, ed., Faith-Based Diplomacy: Trumping Realpolitik, 179.

[311] Sachedina, Abdul Aziz, *The Islamic Roots of Democratic Pluralism*, Oxford, Oxford University Press, 2011, 43-44.

[312] Powell, Islamic Law and International Law, 162–63.

[313] Al-Dawoody, "Islamic Law," 996.
[314] See PBS, "A Historical Timeline of Afghanistan," August 30, 2021, https://www.pbs.org/newshour/politics/asia-jan-june11-timeline-afghanistan (Accessed January 2, 2022).
[315] See for example, Hamid Khan, Opinion Contributor, *Taliban doesn't equal Islam: How News Coverage of Afghanistan Disserves a Great Religion*, USA Today Opinion, August 21, 2021. Taliban and Islam: Why extremism doesn't reflect a great religion (usatoday.com) (Accessed January 2, 2022). See also Tim Foxley and Dr. Antonio Giustozzi, *A Force of Moderation or Radicalisation? The Role of Afghanistan's Ulema | Royal United Services Institute (rusi.org)*, 26 January 2023. (Accessed February 18, 2023).
[316] Mohammad Hashim Kamali, *Against extremism: the middle path of moderation*, Foundazione Oasis, September 13, 2021. https://www.oasiscenter.eu/en/against-extremism-the-middle-path-of-moderation (Accessed January 2, 2022).
[317] Hamid, M. Khan, Islamic Law, Customary Law and Afghan Informal Justice | United States Institute of Peace (usip.org), March 6, 2015. (Accessed 25 September, 2021)
[318] *Islamic Republic of Afghanistan, Constitution of Afghanistan 2004, Article 130.*
[319] *Islamic Republic of Afghanistan, Constitution of Afghanistan 2004, Article 130*
[320] *Islamic Republic of Afghanistan, Constitution of Afghanistan 2004, Article 22.*
[321] *Islamic Republic of Afghanistan, Constitution of Afghanistan 2004, Article 45.*
[322] Powell, *Islamic Law* and *International Law*, 65.
[323] Sohail. H. Hashmi, "Islamic Political Ethics: Civil Society, Pluralism, and Conflict, Princeton University Press, 2002a, 197.
[324] United States Institute of Peace Report, https://www.usip.org/sites/default/files/SR347-Sharia_and_Women%E2%80%99s_Rights_in_Afghanistan.pdf
[325] https://www.amnesty.org.uk/womens-rights-afghanistan-history
[326] Afghanistan Constitution 2004, Article 22.
[327] Afghan Civil Code, 1977, Article 70.
[328] Afghan Civil Code, 1977, Article 71.
[329] USIP Report.
[330] USIP Report.
[331] USIP Report, 2.
[332] Anastasiya Hozyainova, USIP Special Report 347, *Sharia and Women's Rights in Afghanistan."* March 2014, 4. SR347-Sharia_and_Women's_Rights_in_Afghanistan.pdf (usip.org) (Accessed January 2, 2022).
[333] See Ziba Mir-Hosseini, "Muslim Women's Quest for Equality: Between Islamic Law and Feminism," *Critical Inquiry* 32, no. 4 (Summer 2006): 629–645.
[334] Mir-Hosseini, "Muslim Women's Quest," 633.
[335] H. M. Khan, "Islamic Law, Customary Law, and Afghan Informal Justice," *United States Institute of Peace*, https://www.usip.org/publications/2015/03/islamic-law-customary-law-and-afghan-informal-justice (Accessed January 2, 2022).

[336] See Art. 13. *Fundamental Principles of the Democratic Republic of Afghanistan, April, 20, 21 (1980) (SAUR 1, 1359, AH)*, 6-7. Fundamental Principles of the Democratic Republic of Afghanistan: Publication Department, Ministry of Information and Culture, Government Printing House : Free Download, Borrow, and Streaming : Internet Archive (Accessed June 30, 2022).

[337] Anver M. Emon, *Religious Minorities and Islamic Law: Accommodation and the Limits of Tolerance* (Oxford: Oxford University Press), Chapter 19

[338] Julia Schiwal, "Two Futures for Religious Minorities in Afghanistan," LSE Blogs, https://blogs.lse.ac.uk/religionglobalsociety/2021/08/two-futures-for-religious-minorities-in-afghanistan/

[339] Nadjma Yassari, Mohammad Hamid Saboory, *Sharia and National Law in Afghanistan, 2010*. https://www.juragentium.org/topics/islam/en/yassari.htm (Accessed 30 June, 2022). See also *Islamic Republic of Afghanistan, Constitution of Afghanistan 2004, Article 2*.

[340] USIP Report.

[341] Professor Akbar Ahmed, Ibn Khaldun Chair of Islamic Studies, American University, Washington DC, Author Interview with Prof. Akbar Ahmed, 17th December 2022).

[342] See further Akbar Ahmed, Remembering the Wali of Swat (dailytimes.com.pk) June 24, 2020

[343] Professor Akbar Ahmed, Ibn Khaldun Chair of Islamic Studies, American University, Washington DC, Author Interview with Prof. Akbar Ahmed, 17th December 2022.

[344] Sir. T. Beckett, Amb. N. Jamal, Dr. Y. Guzansky, Dr. H. Alhasan, The Abraham Accords: Evolving Partnerships, Persistent Challenges (iiss.org), 27 September 2021 (online event).

[345] See further Tom Beckett, Ambassador Nancy Jamal, Dr Yoel Guzansky, Dr Hasan Alhasan, "The Abraham Accords: Evolving Partnerships, Persistent Challenges (iiss.org)," September 27, 2021.

[346] Khaled Elgindy, *Blind Spot: America and the Palestinians, from Balfour to Trump* (Brookings Institution Press, 2019), 262.

[347] Jewish Agency of Israel, https://archive.jewishagency.org/first-steps/program/5131.

[348] Council on Foreign Relations, https://www.cfr.org/backgrounder/what-know-about-arab-citizens-israel

[349] Council on Foreign Relations.

[350] Author interview with Jonathan Khuttab, International Human Rights Attorney, November 15, 2021.

[351] Elgindy, *Blind Spot*, 1.

[352] United Nations Meeting Coverage, 19 January 2022: https://www.un.org/press/en/2022/sc14769.doc.htm

[353] Elgindy, *Blind Spot*, 5.

[354] Jonathan Kuttab, *Beyond the Two State Solution* (Washington, DC: Nonviolence International, 2021), 33.

[355] Kuttab, *Beyond the Two State Solution*, 36.

[356] Ibid.

[357] Kuttab, *Beyond the Two State Solution*, 35.
[358] Kuttab, *Beyond the Two State Solution*, 68.
[359] Kuttab, *Beyond the Two State Solution*, 37–40.
[360] Kuttab, *Beyond the Two State Solution*, 48.
[361] Kuttab, *Beyond the Two State Solution*, 61.
[362] Article 4, https://www.venice.coe.int/webforms/documents/default.aspx?pdffile=CDL(2009)008-e
[363] See, Schneider, Irene, and Nijmi Edres, eds. *Uses of the Past: Sharī'a and Gender in Legal Theory and Practice in Palestine and Israel*. Lara-Lauren Goudarzi-Gereke, *Perspectives on Palestinian Family Law*, 1st ed. Harrassowitz Verlag, 2018, 47-68. https://doi.org/10.2307/j.ctvcm4fxc/ https://doi.org/10.2307/j.ctvcm4fxc.6.
[364] Majid Khadduri, Book review of Eisenman, Robert H. *Islamic Law in Palestine and Israel: A History of the Survival of Tanzimat and Sharī'a in the British Mandate and the Jewish State*. Vol. 26. Brill, 1978, *Middle East Journal* 33, no. 3 (1979).
[365] Richard Ben Cramer, *How Israel Lost: The Four Questions*, Simon & Schuster, London, 2004, 257.
[366] Cecil J. Hunt II., A Poverty of Respect: Human Rights, Honor, Dignity and Respect in the Israeli-Palestinian Conflict, 71 ALB. L. REV. 2008, 862-3. Citing Richard Ben Cramer, *How Israel Lost: The Four Questions*, Simon & Schuster, London, 2004, 267.
[367] Rodolfo Ragionieri, "The peace process in the Middle East: Israelis and Palestinians," *International Journal of Peace Studies* 2, no. 2 (1997): 49–65, 61.
[368] The State of Palestine is a partially recognised sovereign state, similar to Kosvo and Taiwan, which is currently classified as a "non-member observer state" by the United Nations. As of April 2022, 138 of the UN 193 members (and one observer) have recognised Palestine. The U.S. nor the UK currently recognise the state of Palestine and the latter abstained in the UN GA vote that granted Palestine non-member observer status at the UN. See also UK Government recognition of the State of Palestine alongside the State of Israel - House of Commons Library (parliament.uk), 21 February, 2022.
[369] Office of the United Nations High Commissioner for Human Rights, *Report on the Situation of Human Rights in Kashmir: Developments in the Indian State of Jammu and Kashmir from June 2016 to April 2018, and General Human Rights Concerns in Azad Jammu and Kashmir and Gilgit-Baltistan* (14 June 2018), Accessed 2 January 2022, https://www.ohchr.org/Documents/Countries/PK/DevelopmentsInKashmirJune2016ToApril2018.pdf.
[370] Dalbi· Ahlawat, and M. Raymond Izarali, "India's revocation of Article 370: Security dilemmas and options for Pakistan," *The Round Table* 109, no. 6 (2020): 663–683.
[371] Robi a Khan, Muhammad Zubair Khan, and Zafar Abbas, "Moving towards human cc tastrophe: the abrogation of Article 370 in Kashmir Valley," *Journal of Muslim Minority Affairs* 41, no. 1 (2021): 84.
[372] A militant organisation operating against India in Pakistan. It was founded in 1987 by Hafiz Muhammad Saeed, Abdullah Yusuf Azzam and Zafar Iqbal.

[373] A Pakistan-based, Deobandi-affiliated militant mujahideen group wisely considered a terrorist organisation that has been active in Kashmir since 2000. The group's primary motive is to separate Kashmir from India and merge it into Pakistan.

[374] J. Hayward, *The Leadership of Muhammad: A Historical Reconstruction*, Swansea: Claritas Books, 2021, 115 for analysis of Prophet Muhammad's Diplomatic leadership qualities. Also, author interview with Professor J. Hayward, September 22, 2021 reaffirming the same point.

[375] Quran, 22: 39: "Permission (to fight) has been granted to those for they have been wronged. Verily God has the power to help them."

[376] See further Hayward, *Leadership of Muhammad*. Author interview with Professor J. Hayward, September 22, 2021 which endorsed the same point.

[377] Hayward, *Leadership of Muhammad*.

[378] United Nations Security Council Resolution 39.

[379] The lockdown included preventative measures such as curfew, communication, and media blackout, and an increased Indian military troop presence.

[380] See Caitlin Talmadge, *Are nuclear weapons keeping the India-Pakistan crisis from escalating—or making it more dangerous? (brookings.edu)*, March 8, 2019. (Accessed 18th December 2022).

[381] Asma Afsaruddin, *The Concept of Peace in* Judaism, Christianity and Islam, edited by Georges Tamer, Berlin, Boston: De Gruyter, 2020, 99. https://doi.org/10.1515/9783110682021-003 (Accessed 18th December 2022).

[382] Michael Gottlob, "India's unity in diversity as a question of historical perspective." *Economic and Political Weekly* (2007): 779–789; Singh, Mahendra Pal, and Surya Deva. "The constitution of India: Symbol of unity in diversity," *Jahrbuch des Offentlichen Rechts der Gegenwart, Yearbook of Public Law (Germany)* 53 (2005): 649–686.

[383] *Pseudo* is used to differentiate the Hindutva ideology from the normative tentets of the Hindu faith tradition which would wish to totally disassociate itself from the Hindutva right wing nationalist agenda.

[384] Tanja Herklotz, "Shayara Bano versus Union of India and Others. The Indian Supreme Court's Ban of Triple Talaq and the Debate around Muslim Personal Law and Gender Justice," *Verfassung und Recht in Übersee/Law and Politics in Africa, Asia and Latin America* 50, no. 3 (2017): 300–311.

[385] Ahmed Al-Dawoody, *Respect for the Dead under Islamic Law: Considerations for Humanitarian Forensics,* Humanitarian Law and Policy, https://blogs.icrc.org/law-and-policy/2018/11/01/respect-for-the-dead-under-islamic-law-considerations-for-humanitarian-forensics/ (Accessed 18th December 2022).

[386] Yashraj Sharma, "India is forcing us to pick guns": Kashmir mourns death of 26-yr-old in custody (thekashmirwalla.com), 16 September, 2020. (Accessed 18th December 2022).

[387] *Fahad Shah, Graveyard on a hill: Where do Kashmir's dead go?*, November 2021, https://thekashmirwalla.com/graveyard-on-a-hill-where-do-kashmirs-dead-go/ (Accessed 18th December 2022).

[388] Arendt, Hannah, Editor Jerome Kohn, Essays in Understanding, 1930-1954, Harcourt, Brace & Company, New York,1994, 12.

[389] Kadayifci-Orellana, S. Ayse, Abu-Nimer, and Amjad Mohamed-Saleem. "Understanding an islamic framework for peacebuilding," *Islamic Relief Worldwide, Working Paper Series No* (2013).
[390] Mohammed Abu-Nimer, *Nonviolence and Peace Building in Islam: Theory and practice* (Gainesville: University Press of Florida, 2003).
[391] L. Payne, and Islamic Relief. *Introduction to Peacebuilding: An Islamic Relief Practitioners' Guide* (Stockholm: Islamic Relief Sweden, 2020), 5.
[392] L. Payne, and Islamic Relief. *Introduction to Peacebuilding: An Islamic Relief Practitioners' Guide* (Stockholm: Islamic Relief Sweden, 2020),6.
[393] See further Israel/OPT: Israel is committing apartheid, says UN Special Rapporteur - Amnesty International
[394] See DEC raises £26m as 2022 signals 'unfolding catastrophe' in Afghanistan | Disasters Emergency Committee (Accessed 18th December 2022).
[395] Office of the United Nations High Commissioner for Human Rights Update of the Situation of Human Rights in Indian-Administered Kashmir and Pakistan-Administered Kashmir from May 2018 to April 2019 United Nations (ohchr.org) (Accessed 18th December 2022).
[396] See further Dr. Azeem Ibrahim et al, *The Uyghur Genocide: An Examination of China's Breaches of the 1948 Genocide Convention - New Lines Institute* (Accessed December 18, 2021).
[397] See George Wright, *BBC India offices searched by income tax officials - BBC News* in response to the BBC airing a documentary in the UK *"The Modi Question"* which focuses on the Indian prime ministers role in anti-Muslim violence in Gujrat in 2022, when he was chief minister of the state. (Accessed March 17, 2023).
[398] J. Hayward, *"Justice, Jihad and Duty. The Qur'anic Concept of Armed Conflict," Islam and Civilisational Renewal* 9, no. 3 (2018): 268.
[399] Ahmed al-Dawoody, *"Islamic Law and International Humanitarian Law: An Introduction to the Main Principles,"* International Review of the Red Cross, Vol. 99, nb.3, (2017), 1017. untitled (icrc.org) (Accessed December 19, 2021).
[400] Ahmed al-Dawoody, *"Islamic Law and International Humanitarian Law: An Introduction to the Main Principles,"* International Review of the Red Cross, Vol. 99, nb.3, (2017), 1018. untitled (icrc.org) (Accessed December 19, 2021).
[401] H.R.H. Prince Ghazi bin Muhammad of Jordan, *"A Common Word Between Us and You."* 5-Year Anniversary Edition, MABDA English Monograph Series, No. 20 (The Royal Aal Al Bayt Institute for Islamic Thought, 2012), 7.
[402] Tariq Al-Thaqafi, *"Prominent Muslim Figures: Religious, cultural diversity does not justify "conflict." 31st May 2019.* Prominent Muslim figures: religious, cultural diversity does not justify 'conflict' | Arab News (Accessed December 19, 2021).
[403] Hamza Yusuf, Shaykh, *"Buddha in the Qur'an?"* In *Common Ground Between Islam and Buddhism,* edited by Reza S. Kazemi (Jordan: Fons Vitae, The Royal Aal-Bayt Institute for Islamic Thought, 2010).
[404] See Rifat Fareed *"What to Expect as Kashmir Leaders Meet India's Modi in New Delhi" for a synopsis of the parties involved in the Kashmir dispute." Al Jazeera,* June 24, 2021, https://www.aljazeera.com/news/2021/6/24/what-to-expect-as-kashmiri-leaders-meet-indias-modi)(Accessed December 19, 2021).

[405] A. Hashim and R. Fareed, "Explainer: Who are Kashmir's Armed Groups?" Al Jazeera, March 3, 2019, https://www.aljazeera.com/news/2019/3/3/explainer-who-are-kashmirs-armed-groups (Accessed December 19, 2021)

[406] *J&K Tourism Development Corporation.* "Religions in Kashmir," (2017), https://www.jktdc.co.in/religions-in-kashmir.aspx#:~:text=Christian,%25) and Christianity (0.3%25) (Accessed December 19, 2021)

[407] L. Payne, and Islamic Relief. *Introduction to Peacebuilding: An Islamic Relief Practitioners' Guide* (Stockholm: Islamic Relief Sweden, 2020), 8.

Printed by Amazon Italia Logistica S.r.l.
Torrazza Piemonte (TO), Italy